SUMMON'S MISCELLANY
OF SAINTS AND SINNERS

SUMMON'S MISCELLANY OF SAINTS AND SINNERS

Parminder Summon

WILLIAM B. EERDMANS PUBLISHING COMPANY
GRAND RAPIDS, MICHIGAN / CAMBRIDGE, U.K.

Compilation © 2005 Parminder Summon

First published 2005 in the United Kingdom by
the Canterbury Press Norwich
(a publishing imprint of
Hymns Ancient & Modern Limited,
a registered charity)
9–17 St Albans Place, London N1 0NX

This edition published 2006 in the United States of America by
Wm. B. Eerdmans Publishing Co.
255 Jefferson Ave. S.E., Grand Rapids, Michigan 49503 /
P.O. Box 163, Cambridge CB3 9PU U.K.

Printed in the United States of America

11 10 09 08 07 06   7 6 5 4 3 2 1

ISBN-10 0-8028-3379-9
ISBN-13 978-0-8028-3379-2

www.eerdmans.com

For Neville and Kate

In appreciation of your friendship

CONTENTS

INTRODUCTION

Saint: *A model person of exceptional virtue who has died but whose life and works continue to be excellent examples today.*

Sinner: *An unrepentant and incorrigible transgressor whose behaviour and attitudes display the worst excesses of human nature.*

This book is about champions and villains, knights and knaves, and heaven and hell. The myriad centuries of human history have witnessed many brave men and women, and their counterparts: those bent on evil. The purpose of this book is to inspire and entertain readers by detailing the fascinating lives of saints and the appalling activities of notable sinners. How do we even begin to classify and distinguish between the good and disreputable?

Saints are men and women who have lived their lives and received their reward – the kingdom of God. Their exemplary lives provide us with examples to follow so that we may, in turn, follow them to heaven. 'Feast days' are recognized for many saints. These are very often the day of the year in which they died, especially if they gave up their lives for their faith. These special saints who gave up their lives for their faith are called 'martyrs'. Based on the course of their lives and the circumstances surrounding them, some of the saints serve as 'patrons' of certain peoples, places, ailments and occupations, as they intercede for us before God.

If it is difficult to agree on what makes a saint, in theory it should be much easier to recognize a sinner, for we are all sinners. But what marks out a *notable* sinner? Their character, their environment, their upbringing, their friends, or their time in history, perhaps? Are we born bad or made bad? The reality of evil is perhaps the biggest challenge faced by any individual or society.

As I thought through the subject-matter of this book, I decided to adopt a 'big picture' view of what makes a saint and what characterizes a sinner. This means that people and events presented here are what, to my mind, display in sharp relief the character of saints and sinners.

Most of the insights of a saint come from his or her time as a sinner, for that is our natural state. So we see saints not as remote, ephemeral beings, but real people who went through real trials and emerged inspired by God. Sainthood does not take away the human being, but rather enhances the dust – much as particles caught in sunlight achieve a derived brilliance. We are all clay, but we all have the potential to 'shine like stars'.

So, I trust you will enjoy this diversion into the wonderful world of saints and sinners. We are all sinners but with God's grace we may also know the joy of being his saints!

THE EVE OF ST AGNES

Agnes was a fourth-century Christian virgin and martyr, venerated in both the Eastern and Western Churches. Her story is told in the works of St Jerome, Prudentius, St Ambrose and Pope Damasus I, although there are conflicting versions of her martyrdom.

It is thought that when she was about 14, she refused marriage to a host of suitors because of her dedication to Christ. She was denounced as a Christian during the reign of Diocletian and sent to a house of prostitution as her punishment. When a young man ventured to touch her, he lost his sight, but he then regained it in answer to her prayers. Shortly thereafter she was executed and buried on the Via Nomentana in Rome in a catacomb, and a church was built over her tomb about AD 350.

Her feast day is on 21 January and she is often portrayed with a lamb, a symbol of innocence. To this day, each 21 January, two lambs are blessed at her church in Rome. Their wool is then woven into palliums (bands of white wool), which the Pope confers on archbishops as a token of their jurisdiction.

There are lots of stories surrounding the legend of St Agnes and she has been the subject of paintings, songs and a long poem by John Keats written in 1820. It is said that by performing certain rituals, a virgin might see her true love in a dream on the night of 21 January. These rituals include going without supper; reciting the Paternoster while pulling a row of pins from your sleeve; taking sprigs of rosemary and thyme and sprinkling them with water; and placing a shoe on either side of the bed and saying: 'St Agnes, that's to lovers kind, come, ease the trouble of my mind.'

> They told her how, upon St Agnes' Eve,
> Young virgins might have visions of delight,
> And soft adorings from their loves receive
> Upon the honey'd middle of the night,

If ceremonies due they did aright;
As, supperless to bed they must retire,
And couch supine their beauties, lily white;
Nor look behind, nor sideways, but require
Of Heaven with upward eyes for all that they desire.

Extract from 'The Eve of St Agnes' John Keats

And on sweet St Agnes' night
Please you with the promis'd sight,
Some of husbands, some of lovers,
Which an empty dream discovers.

Ben Jonson

STIGMATICS

Stigma (n. pl. stigmata): *Bodily marks, sores or sensations of pain corresponding in location to the crucifixion wounds of Jesus, usually during states of religious ecstasy or hysteria.*

Stigmatics were unknown before the thirteenth century. Although there is no official list of stigmatics, the Catholic Church recognizes 62 saints or blessed men and women as bearing the marks of Christ. Among the best known are:

St Francis of Assisi (1186–1226)
St Lutgarde (1182–1246)
St Margaret of Cortona (1247–97)
St Gertrude (1256–1302)
St Clare of Montefalco (1268–1308)
Bl Angela of Foligno (d. 1309)
St Catherine of Siena (1347–80)
St Lidwine (1380–1433)
St Frances of Rome (1384–1440)
St Colette (1380–1447)

St Rita of Cassia (1386–1456)
Bl Osanna of Mantua (1499–1505)
St Catherine of Genoa (1447–1510)
Bl Baptista Varani (1458–1524)
Bl Lucy of Narni (1476–1547)
Bl Catherine of Racconigi (1486–1547)
St John of God (1495–1550)
St Catherine de' Ricci (1522–89)
St Mary Magdalene de' Pazzi (1566–1607)
Bl Marie de l'Incarnation (1566–1618)
Bl Mary Anne of Jesus (1557–1620)
Bl Carlo of Sezze (d. 1670)
Blessed Margaret Mary Alacoque (1647–90)
St Veronica Giuliani (1600–1727)
St Mary Frances of the Five Wounds (1715–91)
St Pio of Pietrelcina (Padre Pio) (1887–1968)

THE BARBER SAINT

What is so extraordinary about this man? He radiated a most serene and joyful faith. In the face of constant, painful discrimination he understood, as few have understood, the meaning of the words, 'Father, forgive them; they do not know what they are doing.' No treasure is as uplifting and transforming as the light of faith.

Pope John Paul II, 1995

Born a humble, black slave in Haiti in 1776, Pierre Toussaint was elevated to the status of 'Venerable' by the Pope in 1996. Toussaint lived a remarkable life. With no advantages of wealth or background, he learned to read and write because of his kindly master, Jean Berard.

When the Berard family relocated to New York in 1787, Pierre and his sister Rosalie accompanied them. Pierre trained to be a barber and gained a reputation for his tact and discretion. He refused to spread gossip, even though his customers shared with him many confidences. Instead, he would add their concerns to his growing prayer list so that many people were comforted by his untiring dedication.

When his master died, Toussaint could have obtained his freedom, but instead he continued to support his master's family. Eventually, when Mrs Berard remarried, Toussaint set up his own home and married, but had no children.

The Toussaint home became noted as a haven for orphans and the destitute. Pierre purchased freedom for many slaves, gave generously to establish a school for black children, and helped to set up a religious order for black women in Baltimore. He didn't perform miracles, write great books, experience mystical visions or institute a new philosophy. He was an ordinary man, made extraordinary by his faith. Born in the injustice of slavery, Toussaint never allowed his poverty to rob him of his dignity. He rose above racist slurs and ignorant attitudes. He was content to work as a humble barber for God. He did not know the benefits of a privileged birth, but experienced the depths of a generous heart, a confident faith and a close walk with his Saviour.

Toussaint died in 1853 and many poor people who had been helped by his generous life came to pay tribute to him. Today, he is the only layman buried in St Patrick's Cathedral in New York, alongside bishops, cardinals and priests.

Towards the end of his life, Toussaint observed, 'Jesus can give you nothing so precious as himself, as his own mind. Do not think that any faith in him can do you good if you do not try to be pure and true like him.'

THE SAINT MAKER

Archbishop Karol Joseph Wojtyla became Pope John Paul II on 16 October 1978. His death on 2 April 2005 marked the end of the third longest papal reign after Pope Pius IX and the Apostle Peter. Among other things, Pope John Paul II is remembered as a great communicator and tireless traveller, and during his pontificate he canonized more people than any other Pope.

Included in the list of believers made saints by John Paul II are:

Saint	Role	Canonized
Josemaría Escrivá de Balaguer (1902–75)	Founder of Opus Dei	October 2002
Pio da Pietrelcina (1887–1968)	Capuchin priest	June 2002
Edith Stein (1891–1942)	Carmelite martyr	October 1998
Thérèse of Lisieux (1873–97)	Doctor of the Church	June 1997 (originally May 1925)
Maximilian Maria Kolbe (1894–1941)	World War Two martyr	October 1982
Giuseppe Moscati (1880–1927)	Scientist	October 1987
Magdalena of Canossa (1774–1835)	Founder of the of Canossian Family of Daughters and Sons of Charity	October 1988
Clelia Barbieri (1847–70)	Founder of the religious community 'Suore Minime dell'Addolorata'	April 1989

Gaspar Bertoni (1777–1853)	Founder of the Congregation of the Sacred Stigmata of Our Lord Jesus Christ	November 1989
Claudine Thévenet (1774–1837)	Founder of the Congregation of the Religious of Jesus and Mary	March 1993
Hedwig (1374–99)	Queen of Poland	June 1997
John Calabria (1873–1954)	Founder of the Congregation of the Poor Servants and the Poor Women Servants of Divine Providence	April 1999

HOLY NUDISM

The Adamites were an obscure sect that probably originated in North Africa in the second century. They had some strange practices arising from their foundational belief: that they had discovered what life was like before Adam and Eve sinned. They claimed to have returned to a life of innocence before the corruption of sin arising from man's downfall.

Their meetings must have been interesting because they worshipped without clothes (as Adam and Eve had been naked in the Garden of Eden), encouraged freedom of sexual expression and forbade marriage. Their church was called 'paradise', they lived communally, and they frowned upon private possessions.

From North Africa, the sect spread to Spain and Bohemia, but they never gained a large following. In the fourteenth century, the Adamites resurfaced in Eastern Europe as the Brothers and Sisters of the Free Spirit (also known as the

Picards). In the pre-Reformation period, it is thought that the Adamites gradually died out as other sects took hold.

However, in the English Civil War period, around 1650, the Adamites resurfaced again around London. This was a period of great upheaval and their teaching that they were above human laws was attractive to some. They believed they were in a divine state of grace and therefore not beholden to civil, moral or social restraints. It is thought that this sect was dominated by women, but there is scant evidence of their lives from their own accounts. After the Restoration in 1660, the sect died out.

APOSTLE SPOONS

As St Paul's Day, 25 January, is the first feast day of an apostle in the year, it was an old English custom to present spoons (known as apostle spoons) at christenings. The apostle spoons were a gift of 12 spoons with figures of all the apostles on them. Poor people gave one spoon to the child with the figure of the saint after whom the child was named, or to whom the child was dedicated.

This custom is alluded to in Ben Jonson's *Bartholomew Fair*, where a character says, 'And all this for the hope of a couple of apostle-spoons, and a cup to eat caudle in.'

Today these apostle spoons are of considerable value to collectors. The illustration above shows a typical set of such spoons.

FOURTEEN HOLY HELPERS

In the fourteenth century, the Black Plague devastated Europe and many died without receiving the last sacraments. It was a violent time, and those with the disease were often attacked and segregated.

Many people invoked a group of saints known as the Fourteen Holy Helpers during the Black Plague. Their devotion began in Germany and spread throughout most of Europe during the fourteenth century. The Fourteen Holy Helpers collectively venerated on 8 August every year were:

Saint	Condition
Achatius	Headaches
Barbara	Fevers, sudden death
Blaise	Ills of the throat
Catherine of Alexandria	Sudden death
Christopher	Plagues, sudden death
Cyriacus	Temptation
Denis	Headaches
George	Protection of domestic animals
Giles	Plagues
Margaret of Antioch	For safe childbirth
Pantaleon	Protection of domestic animals
Vitus	Epilepsy
Erasmus	Intestinal trouble
Eustachius	Difficult situations

Invocation of the Holy Helpers

Fourteen Holy Helpers, who served God in humility and confidence on earth and are now in the enjoyment of His beatific vision in Heaven; because thou persevered till death thou gained the crown of eternal life. Remember the dangers that surround us in this vale of tears, and intercede for us in all our needs and adversities. Amen.

Fourteen Holy Helpers, select friends of God, I honour thee as mighty intercessors, and come with filial confidence to thee in my needs, for the relief of which I have undertaken to make this novena. Help me by thy intercession to placate God's wrath, which I have provoked by my sins, and aid me in amending my life and doing penance. Obtain for me the grace to serve God with a willing heart, to be resigned to His holy will, to be patient in adversity and to persevere unto the end, so that, having finished my earthly course, I may join thee in Heaven, there to praise for ever God, who is wonderful in His Saints. Amen.

Catholic Encyclopaedia, Robert Appleton, 1907

NUREMBERG TRIALS

After World War II, on 20 November 1945, the Allies convened an International Military Tribunal at the Palace of Justice in Nuremberg, in Germany, to prosecute Nazi war criminals.

The indictment that served as the basis for the trials and for charging the defendants contained four counts:

Count One – The Common Plan or Conspiracy to wage a aggressive war in violation of international law or treaties.

Count Two – Planning, preparation, or waging an aggressive war.

Count Three – War Crimes – violations of the international rules of war (mistreatment of prisoners of war or civilian populations, the plunder of private property and the destruction of towns and cities without military justification).

Count Four – Crimes Against Humanity – murder, extermination, enslavement of civilian populations; persecution on the basis of racial, religious or political grounds.

The defendants (and their fate) are:

Name	Fate
Hermann Goering	Sentenced to death, but committed suicide
Rudolph Hess	Life imprisonment – committed suicide in 1987
Hans Frank	Sentenced to death
Wilhelm Frick	Sentenced to death
Julius Streicher	Sentenced to death
Walther Funk	Life imprisonment – died in 1960
Fritz Sauckel	Sentenced to death
Alfred Jodl	Sentenced to death
Martin Bormann	Sentenced to death (in absentia)
Franz von Papen	Acquitted
Joachim von Ribbentrop	Sentenced to death
Wilhelm Keitel	Sentenced to death
Ernst Kaltenbrunner	Sentenced to death
Alfred Rosenberg	Sentenced to death
Hjalmar Schacht	Acquitted
Karl Doenitz	10 years' imprisonment
Erich Raeder	Life imprisonment
Baldur von Schirach	20 years' imprisonment
Arthur Seyss-Inquart	Sentenced to death
Albert Speer	20 years' imprisonment
Konstantin von Neurath	15 years' imprisonment
Hans Fritzsche	Acquitted

The Trials concluded on 1 October 1946, the Jewish Day of Atonement.

WITCHCRAFT IN SALEM COUNTY

The principal parties accused of witchcraft in Salem County, Massachusetts, in 1692 and their fate were:

Accused	Sentence
Sarah Osborn	Died in prison
Roger Toothaker	Died in prison
Lydia Dustin	Died in prison
Ann Foster	Died in prison
Bridget Bishop	Executed 10 June 1692
Rebecca Nurse	Executed 19 July 1692
Sarah Good	Executed 19 July 1692
Susannah Martin	Executed 19 July 1692
Elizabeth Howe	Executed 19 July 1692
Sarah Wildes	Executed 19 July 1692
John Willard	Executed 19 August 1692
George Jacobs, Sr	Executed 19 August 1692
John Proctor	Executed 19 August 1692
George Burroughs	Executed 19 August 1692
Martha Carrier	Executed 19 August 1692
Giles Corey	Pressed to death 16 September 1692
Marth Corey	Executed 22 September 1692
Mary Easty	Executed 22 September 1692
Ann Pudeator	Executed 22 September 1692
Alice Parker	Executed 22 September 1692

Mary Parker	Executed 22 September 1692
Wilmott Redd	Executed 22 September 1692
Margaret Scott	Executed 22 September 1692
Samuel Wardwell	Executed 22 September 1692

'SAINTS GO MALTING IN'

It is strange to note that many saints have ancient connections with the production of beer. Here is a list of saints and their links with beer:

Saint	Brewing link
Lawrence	He suffered martyrdom in 258 by being strapped to a grid iron that was slowly roasted over an open flame. He is remembered by brewers because this is how malt is dried.
Dorothy	Died in 311 after undergoing similar tortures to St Lawrence. Remembered for the same reason by brewers.
Augustine of Hippo	Known for his wild living (including drunkenness) prior to his conversion. He is the patron saint of brewers.
Luke the Apostle	Another patron of brewers, possibly due to his being a doctor and recommending beer as a useful medium in which to mix herbs for medicinal purposes.
Nicholas of Myra	The model for Santa Claus is supposed to have revived three church scholars in an inn. He is therefore the protector of travellers and brewers.

Wenceslas	Said to have imposed the death penalty on anyone caught exporting Bohemian hops. Remembered by hop-growers, and is the patron saint of Czech brewers. He is the ancestor of Wenceslas II who, in the thirteenth century, convinced the Pope to lift the ban on the brewing of beer.
Veronus	The patron saint of Belgian brewers.
Brigid	She is supposed to have bathed lepers in beer.
Amand	Considered the father of Belgian monasticism, he established many beer-producing monasteries across northern France and Belgium.
Gambrinus	The legendary King of Flanders, he is also known as the 'King of Beer', for reputedly inventing hopped, malt beer.
Arnold of Soissons	The patron saint of hop pickers because he preached in the hop-laden areas of Brabant.
Arnold of Metz	According to legend, he ended a plague when he submerged his crucifix into a brew kettle and persuaded people to drink only beer from that 'blessed' kettle. He is reported to have said, 'From man's sweat and God's love, beer came into the world'.

FAMOUS FRAUDSTERS

'Count' Victor Lustig	In 1925 he tried to sell the Eiffel Tower to scrap merchants.
Frank Abagnale	Famous forger and impersonator, portrayed by Leonardo di Caprio in the film *Catch Me If You Can*.
Marmaduke Wetherell and Colonel Robert Wilson	Responsible for the famous fake Loch Ness Monster photo.
Charles Ponzi	Inventor of the 'pyramid scheme'.
Joseph 'Yellow Kid' Weil	The inspiration for hit film *The Sting*.
Clifford Irving	Fake 'autobiography' of Howard Hughes.
John Stonehouse	UK politician who faked his own death in 1974.
Charles Dawson	Piltdown Man hoax.
George Hull	Fake prehistoric figure, the Cardiff Giant.
Mahzer Mahmood	Fake 'Tabloid' sheik who had conversations with Sophie Rhys-Jones, wife of Prince Edward.
Charles Redheffer	Inventor of a perpetual motion machine.
Mary Baker	Fake Oriental – Princess Caraboo.
William Henry Ireland	Faked Shakespeare's relics.
Frances Griffiths and Elsie Wright	Photographed the so-called Cottingley Fairies.

Richard Dimbleby	Presenter of the famous April Fool's joke of the Swiss spaghetti harvest on *Panorama* in 1957.
Konrad Kujau	Fake Hitler diaries.

THE GOVERNMENT OF HADES

In 1583, German physician and occultist Johannes Wierus published a major work called *Pseudomonarchia Daemonum*, which attempted to detail the Government of Hades. According to Wierus, the chief emperor of the demons was Belzebuth or Belzebub. He is said to have been worshipped by the people of Canaan in the form of a fly, and hence believed to have founded the Order of the Fly. Wierus claimed that Satan, the former emperor, had been usurped and was now the leader of the opposition.

Wierus included the following evil spirits in the Government of Hades:

Name	Title
Eurynome	Prince of Death
Moloch	Prince of the Country of Tears
Pluto	Prince of Fire
Baalberith	Secretary General of the Archives of Hell
Prosperine	Princess of Evil Spirits
Belphegor	Hadean Ambassador to France
Mammon	Hadean Ambassador to England
Belial	Hadean Ambassador to Turkey
Rimmon	Hadean Ambassador to Russia
Thammuz	Hadean Ambassador to Spain
Hutgin	Hadean Ambassador to Italy

Martinet	Hadean Ambassador to Switzerland
Lucifer	Minister of Justice
Alastor	Executioner

Wierus calculated that Belzebuth's Empire had 6,666 legions, each composed of 6,666 demons, giving a Hadean population of over 44 million.

JOSEPH SCRIVEN

Joseph Scriven was the author of the popular hymn 'What a Friend We Have in Jesus'. An exemplary Christian, born in Ireland in 1819, Scriven emigrated to Canada following a tragedy. He was due to marry a local girl, but in 1842, on the eve of their wedding, his fiancée drowned in the River Bann after falling from her horse.

The incident that inspired the hymn occurred in 1854. Joseph was again due to be married in 1854 to Elizabeth Roche. Unfortunately, she caught a chill, became seriously ill, and died after suffering for three years. Scriven was extremely moved by these events and wrote the hymn orginally as a poem for his mother in 1857. It was originally called 'Pray Without Ceasing' .

What a Friend We Have in Jesus

What a friend we have in Jesus,
All our sins and griefs to bear!
What a privilege to carry
Everything to God in prayer!
O what peace we often forfeit,
O what needless pain we bear,
All because we do not carry
Everything to God in prayer.

Have we trials and temptations?
  Is there trouble anywhere?
We should never be discouraged
  Take it to the Lord in prayer!
Can we find a friend so faithful,
Who will all our sorrows share?
Jesus knows our every weakness
  Take it to the Lord in prayer!

Are we weak and heavy laden,
Cumbered with a load of care?
Precious Saviour, still our refuge
  Take it to the Lord in prayer.
Do your friends despise forsake you?
  Take it to the Lord in prayer!
In His arms He'll take and shield you
  You will find a solace there.

SAINTS AND WEATHER LORE

St Vincent's Day – 22 January

St Vincent was a Spanish martyr who died in 304 after suffering torture by fire. An ancient proverb says that if the sun is out on St Vincent's Day, then it will continue to shine throughout the rest of the month:

Remember on St Vincent's Day
If that the sun his beams display.

St Paul's Day – 25 January

According to *Every-Day Book*, 1825–7, 'On this day prognostications of the months were drawn for the whole year. If fair and clear, there was to be plenty; if cloudy or misty, much cattle would die; if rain or snow fell then it presaged a dearth; and if windy, there would be wars:'

> If Saint Paul's Day be fair and clear.
> It does betide a happy year;
> But if it chance to snow or rain,
> Then will be dear all kinds of grain:
> If clouds or mists do dark the skie,
> Great store of birds and beasts shall die;
> And if the winds do fly aloft,
> Then wars shall vex the kingdome oft.

Candlemass Day – 2 February

This feast day celebrates the purification of the Virgin Mary, 40 days after the birth of Jesus. The weather on this day is said to mark the progress of winter according to the rhyme:

> If the sun shines bright on Candlemass Day
> The half of Winter's not yet away

St Winwaloe's Day – 3 March

St Winwaloe's Day is associated with storms, according to this rhyme:

> First there's David
> Then there's Chad
> Next comes Winwaloe
> Roaring mad

St Medard's Day – 8 June

> Should Saint Medard's day be wet
> It will rain for forty yet;
> At least until Saint Barnabas

The summer sun won't favour us,
If on the eighth of June it rain,
It foretells a wet harvest, men sain.

Saints Gervasius and Protasius – 19 June

S'il pleut le jour de Saint Médard,
Il pleut quarante jours plus tard;
S'il pleut le jour de Saint Gervais
    et de Saint Protais,
Il pleut quarante jours après.

St Swithin's Day – 15 July

In this month is St Swithin's Day;
On which, if that it rain, they say
Full forty days after it will,
Or more or less, some rain distill.
This Swithin was a saint, I trow,
And Winchester's bishop also.
Who in his time did many a feat,
As popish legends do repeat:
A woman having broke her eggs
By stumbling at another's legs,
For which she made a woful cry,
St Swithin chanc'd for to come by,
Who made them all as sound, or more
Than ever that they were before.
But whether this were so or no
'Tis more than you or I do know:
Better it is to rise betime,
And to make hay while sun doth shine,
Than to believe in tales and lies
Which idle monks and friars devise.

St James's Day – 25 July

If it be fair three Sundays before St James Day, corn will be good; but wet corn will wither

St Andrew's Day – 30 November

According to an old country saying, '*St Andrew's snow to corn works woe*'

Hone's Every-Day Book, *1825–27*

DOCTORS OF THE CHURCH

The Catholic Church proclaims a person to be a Doctor of the Church if they meet three requirements according to Pope Benedict XIV's definition: an eminent doctrine, a remarkable holiness of life, and the declaration by the Supreme Pontiff or by a General Council.

Below is a list of Doctors of the Church, starting with their name(s), the Pope who proclaimed them, and the date on which this occurred:

- 1–4: Saints Ambrose, Jerome, Augustine, Gregory the Great: Boniface VIII, 20 September 1295.
- 5: Saint Thomas Aquinas: Saint Pius V, 11 April 1567.
- 6–9: Saints Athanasius, Basil, Gregory of Nazianzus, Saint John Chrysostom: Saint Pius V, 1568.
- 10: Saint Bonaventure: Sixtus V, 14 March 1588.
- 11: Saint Anselm of Canterbury: Clement XI, 3 February 1720.
- 12: Saint Isidore of Seville: Innocent XIII, 25 April 1722.
- 13: Saint Peter Chrysologus: Benedict XIII, 10 February 1729.
- 14: Saint Leo the Great: Benedict XIV, 15 October 1754.
- 15: Saint Peter Damian: Leo XII, 27 September 1828.
- 16: Saint Bernard of Clairvaux: Pius VIII, 20 August 1830.
- 17: Saint Hilaire of Poitiers: Pius IX, 13 May 1851.
- 18: Saint Alphonsus Liguori: Pius IX, 7 July 1871.

- 19: Saint Francis of Sales: Pius IX, 16 November 1871.
- 20–21: Saints Cyril of Alexandria and Cyril of Jerusalem: Leo XIII, 28 July 1882.
- 22: Saint John Damascene: Leo XIII, 19 August 1890.
- 23: Saint Bede the Venerable: Leo XIII, 13 November 1899.
- 24: Saint Ephrem of Syria: Benedict XV, 5 October 1920.
- 25: Saint Peter Canisius: Pius XI, 21 May 1925.
- 26: Saint John of the Cross: Pius XI, 24 August 1926.
- 27: Saint Robert Bellarmine: Pius XI, 17 September 1931.
- 28: Saint Albert the Great: Pius XI, 16 December 1931.
- 29: Saint Antony of Padua: Pius XII, 16 January 1946.
- 30: Saint Laurence of Brindisi: John XXIII, 19 March 1959.
- 31: Saint Teresa of Avila: Paul VI, 27 September 1970.
- 32: Saint Catherine of Siena: Paul VI, 4 October 1970.
- 33: Saint Thérèse of Lisieux: John Paul II, 19 October 1997.

CURIOUS SAINTS DAY CUSTOMS

- In Scotland, on the eve of St Andrew's Day (29 November), the traditional sport was squirrel hunting. This 'Andermas' custom was transported to the colonies and still survives in some parts of the Commonwealth.
- In Poland, if there is a red sunset on St Nicholas's Day (6 December), it is thought that angels are making his favourite honey cakes.
- Assumption Day (15 August) is reckoned to be an excellent time for betrothals in Brittany.
- In Spain, on St Giles's Day (1 September) rams were dyed in bright colours and blessed in special church services. As well as being the saint of cripples, St Giles is also known as the protector of rams.
- On St George's Day (23 April), races, processions and jousts were held in medieval England.
- On St Hugh's Day (1 April), mock turtle soup is traditionally eaten in Switzerland. This recalls the saint's transformation of a bowl of fowl into turtles!

- Traditionally, Welshmen wear leeks in their hats on St David's Day (1 March).
- In the Middle Ages, it was thought that birds began to mate on St Valentine's Day (14 February).
- Sheaves of corn used to be hung decoratively over church doors on Lammas Day (1 August) – the feast of St Peter – to mark the reaping of the first fruits.

SAINT-RELATED PHRASES

St Andrew's Cross	An X-shaped cross, like the one upon which St Andrew suffered martyrdom. Also the name of a low-growing North American shrub.
St Antony's Cross	A T-shaped cross, like the one upon which St Antony suffered martyrdom.
St Antony's Fire	An acute inflammatory skin disease, so called because St Antony was supposed to have cured a sufferer from it. Also known as erysipelas.
St Antony's Nut	*Conopodium mais,* a groundnut used for swinefeed. St Antony was once a swineherd.
St Antony's Turnip	Another favourite food of swine, popularly known as the bulbous crowfoot.
St Barnaby's Thistle	Supposed to flower on St Barnabas's Day (11 June), this is a kind of knapweed (*Centaurea solstitialis).*
St Catherine's Flower	The plant commonly known as 'love in a mist'.

St Cuthbert's Beads	A paleontological term used to describe the crinoid stems of fossil joints.
St Cuthbert's Duck	A species of eider duck.
St Dabeoc's Heath	Named after an Irish saint, this is a heather-like plant found in Ireland (*Daboecia polifolia*).
St David's Herb	*Allium porrum*, the leek is David's emblem.
St Distaff's Day	Also known as Rock Day, this is the day after Epiphany (7 January). So called because it marked the day when work began after the Christmas feast.
St Elmo's Fire	A luminous flame seen on a ship, probably caused by a discharge of electricity. St Elmo is the patron of sailors.
St George's Ensign	A red cross on a white field with the Union Jack in the upper corner next to the mast. It is the badge of the English Royal Navy.
St George's Flag	A red cross upon a white field. Its presence on a ship is used to indicate that the vessel is under the command of an admiral.
St George's Flower	*Endymion non-scriptus*, the blue-bell that reaches its peak around St George's Day, 23 April.
St George's Herb	The plant commonly known as valerian.
St Gregory's Fig	*Ficus carica* – figs were given on St Gregory's Day to schoolchildren at the Free School in Giggleswick, Yorkshire.

St Ignatius's Bean	The seed from a tree native to the Philippines (*Strychnos ignatia*).
St James's Shell	A comb (pecten) worn by pilgrims to Compostella.
St James's Wort	A kind of ragwort (*Senecio jacobaea*).
St John's Bread	*Ceratonia siliqua,* the locust tree or carob.
St John's Wort	Any plant of the genus *Hypericum.*
St Joseph's Flower	*Althaea rosea,* Holyoake – traditionally planted on St Joseph's Day
St Johnstone's Tippet	Hangman's noose.
St Leger	A horse race named after Colonel St Leger.
St Martin's Herb	A medicinal herb from Latin America, *Sayvagesia erecta.*
St Michael's Chair	Stone feature on St Michael's Mount in Cornwall.
St Monday	Day of idleness observed by workers such as shoemakers and merchants.

ALL SAINTS' DAY

This day honours all saints of the Church, even those not known by name. The first All Saints' Day occurred on 13 May AD 609, although Ephrem Syrus mentions a feast dedicated to saints taking place in the fourth century. In the same century, St Chrysostom of Constantinople assigned All Saints' Day to the first Sunday after Pentecost. It was not recognized in the Western Church, however, until the Roman bishop

Boniface IV consecrated the Pantheon at Rome to Christian usage as a church on 13 May 609. All Saints' Day was observed annually on this date until Pope Gregory III changed the date to 1 November, since on this date he dedicated a chapel in the Basilica of St Peter's to 'All the Saints' in the seventh century. The Orthodox Churches still observe All Saints Day on the first Sunday after Pentecost.

All Saints Day is celebrated by Roman Catholics, Orthodox Churches, Anglicans and Lutherans. However, different denominations celebrate the day for different reasons. For Roman Catholics, Orthodox Churches and, to some extent, Anglicans, All Saints' Day is a day to venerate and pray to the saints in heaven. For Lutherans, the day is observed by remembering and thanking God for all saints, both dead and living.

FAMOUS SAINTS' PRAYERS

A Prayer of St Francis

> Lord, make me an instrument of thy peace,
> Where there is hatred, let me sow love;
> Where there is injury, pardon;
> Where there is doubt, faith;
> Where there is despair, hope;
> Where there is darkness, light;
> Where there is sadness, joy.
> O Divine Master,
> Grant that I may not so much seek
> To be consoled, as to console;
> To be understood, as to understand;
> To be loved, as to love;
> For it is in giving that we receive;
> It is in pardoning that we are pardoned;
> And it is in dying that we are
> born to eternal life. Amen.

St Patrick's Breastplate

May the strength of God pilot us.
May the power of God preserve us.
May the wisdom of God instruct us.
May the hand of God protect us.
May the way of God direct us.
May the shield of God defend us,
May the host of God guard us
Against the snares of evil
  and the temptations of the world.
May Christ be with us, Christ before us,
Christ in us, Christ over us.
May thy salvation, O Lord, be always ours
this day and evermore.

St Anselm's Prayer

O Lord our God, grant us grace to desire thee with our
  whole heart;
that so desiring, we may seek and find thee;
and finding thee, we may love thee;
and loving thee, we may hate those sins from which thou
  hast redeemed us.

Ignatius Loyola's Prayer

Teach us, good Lord, to serve thee as thou deservest;
to give and not to count the cost;
to fight and not to heed the wounds;
to toil and not to seek for rest;
to labour and not to ask for any reward,
save that of knowing we do thy will. Amen.

CLASSIFICATION OF SAINTS

Orthodox Church classification:

Apostles	Those who were chosen by Jesus and witnessed his ministry.
Prophets	Those who predicted the coming of the Messiah.
Martyrs	Those who sacrifice their lives for their faith in Christ.
Church Fathers	Those who excel in explaining and defending the faith.
Monastics	Desert dwellers dedicated to spiritual excellence.
Just	Those who live exemplary lives in testimony to Christ.

BECOMING A SAINT

In the Catholic Church, canonization – the process the Church uses to elect a saint – was clarified by Pope John Paul II in 1983. Previously, saints were chosen by public acclaim. Though this was a more democratic way to recognize saints, some saints' stories were distorted by legend and some supposed saints never existed. As a result, gradually the bishops – and finally the Vatican – took over authority for canonization.

Today, canonization begins after the death of a Catholic whom people regard as holy. Often, the process starts many years after their death in order to give perspective to the candidate. The local bishop investigates the candidate's life and writings for heroic virtue (or martyrdom) and orthodoxy of doctrine. Then a panel of theologians at the Vatican evaluates the candidate. Upon the recommendation of the panel and cardinals of the Congregation for the Causes of Saints, the Pope proclaims the candidate *venerable*.

The next step, *beatification*, requires evidence of one miracle (except in the case of martyrs). Since miracles are considered proof that the person is in heaven and can intercede for us, the miracle must take place after the candidate's death and as a result of a specific petition to the candidate. When the Pope proclaims the candidate beatified or 'blessed', the person can be venerated by a particular region or group of people for whom the person holds special importance.

After one more miracle the Pope will canonize the saint (this includes martyrs as well). The title of 'saint' tells us that the person lived a holy life, is in heaven, and is to be honoured by the Church.

Though canonization is infallible and irrevocable, it takes a long time and a lot of effort. So while every person who is canonized is a saint, not every holy person has been canonized.

LAST WORDS AT EXECUTION

You are going to hurt me, please don't hurt me, just one more moment, I beg you!

[*Guillotined*] – Madame du Barry, mistress of Louis XV, d. 1793

Take a step forward, lads. It will be easier that way.

[*Executed by firing squad*] – Erskine Childers, Irish patriot, d. 24 November 1922

Such is life

[*Executed by hanging*] – Ned Kelly, Australian bushranger, d. 1880

Farewell, my children, forever. I go to your Father.

[*Executed by guillotine*]
Monsieur, I beg your pardon.

[*Spoken to the executioner, after she stepped on his foot*] –
Marie Antoinette, Queen of France, d. 16 October 1793

Shoot me in the chest!

[*To his executioners*] – Benito Mussolini, Italian dictator,
d. 1945

So the heart be right, it is no matter which way the head
lieth.

[*Executed by beheading*] – Sir Walter Raleigh, d. 29 October
1618

OUR LADY OF HATRED

(Fr. Notre-Dame de la Haine)

The name popularly given to a church in Treguier, Brittany.
Souvestre, in his *Derniers Bretons*, vol. i, p. 92, tells us that
'hither come at even-tide young people tired of the surveillance
of their elders, old men envious of the prosperity of their
neighbours, wives chafing under the despotism of their
husbands, each praying for the death of the object of their
hate. Three Aves, devoutly repeated, will bring about this
death within the twelve-month.'

Curiosities of Popular Customs and of Rites, Ceremonies,
Observances, and Miscellaneous Antiquities, *William S. Walsh, J. B.
Lippincott Company*, 1852

Anthony Trollope's older brother, Thomas, wrote many
novels, mostly based in Italy. His autobiography, *What I
Remember* (1887), contrasts some of his recollections of child-

hood with those of his younger brother Anthony. This is his account of his visit to Brittany, where he too heard about Our Lady of Hatred.

Very near Treguier, on a spot appropriately selected for such a worship – the barren top of a bleak unsheltered eminence – stands the chapel of Notre Dame de la Haine! Our Lady of HATRED! The most fiendish of human passions is supposed to be under the protection of Christ's religion! What is this but a fragment of pure and unmixed Paganism, unchanged except in the appellation of its idol, which has remained among these lineal descendants of the Armorican Druids for more than a thousand years after Christianity has become the professed religion of the country! Altars, professedly Christian, were raised under the protection of the Protean Virgin, to the demon Hatred; and have continued to the present day to receive an unholy worship from blinded bigots, who hope to obtain Heaven's patronage and assistance for thoughts and wishes which they would be ashamed to breathe to man. Three Aves repeated with devotion at this odious and melancholy shrine are firmly believed to have the power to cause, within the year, the certain death of the person against whom the assistance of Our Lady of Hatred has been invoked. And it is said that even yet occasionally, in the silence and obscurity of the evening, the figure of some assassin worshipper at this accursed shrine may be seen to glide rapidly from the solitary spot, where he has spoken the unhallowed prayer whose mystic might has doomed to death the enemy he hates.

What I Remember, *Thomas Adolphous Trollope, 1887*

THE WICKED LADY

Katherine Ferrers, lady by day, highway robber by night, and known as the 'Wicked Lady', has been the subject of fascination for over 300 years. Born in 1634 during the English Civil War, Ferrers was heir to a large fortune until she was cheated out of it by circumstances beyond her control.

Her father, Knighton Ferrers, died just two weeks before she was born. Her mother, Lady Katherine Walters of Hertingford, remarried Sir Simon Fanshaw, a noted royalist, who purloined the family fortune and had to go into hiding in Europe. Thus Katherine Ferrers was denied her family inheritance.

According to legend, around 1652 Katherine met a farmer, Ralph Chaplin, who was a highwayman by night. She joined Chaplin and wrought havoc on travellers in the Hertfordshire countryside. One night, Chaplin was caught committing a robbery and executed on the spot.

Lady Katherine Ferrers became a solitary robber dressed in highwayman's garb: a three-cornered hat, a black mask, black riding cloak, scarf and breeches, and rode a black horse with white flashes on its forelegs. She would change at dusk into her highwayman's clothes in a secret room in her house, accessed through a concealed staircase. She did not use the standard 'Stand and deliver' charge to her victims, but emerged from the darkness to ruthlessly attack coachmen and passengers alike. Yet nobody, not even her servants, knew of Katherine's misdeeds.

Lady Katherine has been caricatured as a pretty young woman wearing a black mask over her eyes, perhaps with a roguish smile, or simply as a stereotyped masked highwayman, indistinguishable from her male peers. Always there is the gun and the three-cornered hat.

Among the crimes attributed to the Wicked Lady were murder, robbery, arson, cattle who were shot in the fields, and a policeman who was shot dead on his own doorstep.

The Wicked Lady died childless in 1660 and was buried in Ware, Hertfordshire.

Her story has been the basis of at least two films, a novel by Sir Walter Scott and countless ballads. It is said that the ghost of the Wicked Lady can be still seen today as a figure astride a galloping black horse in the Hertfordshire countryside on bleak winter nights.

PRINCIPAL NATIONAL SAINTS

Nation	Saint	Memorial Day
Albania	Our Lady of Good Counsel	26 April
Algeria	Cyprian of Carthage	16 September
Angola	Immaculate Heart of Mary	22 August
Argentina	Francis Solano	14 July
Armenia	Gregory the Illuminator	30 September
Australia	Francis Xavier	3 December
Austria	Florian	4 May
Belgium	Columbanus of Ghent	2 February
Bolivia	Francis Solano	14 July
Brazil	Antony of Padua	13 June
Bulgaria	Cyril the Philosopher	14 February
Chile	Francis Solano	14 July
China	Francis Xavier	3 December
Costa Rica	Our Lady of The Angels	2 August
Cuba	Our Lady of Charity of El Cobre	8 September
Cyprus	Barnabas the Apostle	11 June
Czech Rep.	Wenceslas	28 September
Denmark	Canute	19 January
Dominican Rep.	Dominic de Guzman	8 August
Egypt	Mark the Evangelist	25 April

Ethiopia	Frumentius	27 October
England	George	23 April
France	Joan of Arc	30 May
Germany	Boniface	5 June
Gibraltar	Bernard of Clairvaux	20 August
Greece	Andrew the Apostle	30 November
Guatemala	James the Greater	25 July
Haiti	Our Lady of Perpetual Help	27 June
Hungary	Astricus	12 November
Iceland	Thorlac Thorhallsson	23 December
India	Thomas the Apostle	3 July
Iran	Maruthas	4 December
Ireland	Patrick	17 March
Italy	Our Lady of Perpetual Help	27 June
Jamaica	Mary of the Assumption	15 August
Japan	Francis Xavier	3 December
Jordan	John the Baptist	24 June
Korea	Joseph the Betrothed	19 March
Lithuania	Casimir of Poland	4 March
Luxembourg	Philip the Apostle	3 May
Madagascar	Vincent de Paul	27 September
Malta	Paul the Apostle	25 January
Mexico	Elias del Socorro Nieves	10 March
Netherlands	Bavo	1 October

New Zealand	Francis Xavier	3 December
Nicaragua	James the Greater	25 July
Nigeria	Patrick	17 March
Norway	Olaf II	29 July
Pakistan	Thomas the Apostle	3 July
Papua New Guinea	Michael the Archangel	29 September
Paraguay	Francis Solano	14 July
Peru	Francis Solano	14 July
Philippines	Rose of Lima	23 August
Poland	Casimir of Poland	4 March
Romania	Nicetas	7 January
Russia	Andrew the Apostle	30 November
Scotland	Andrew the Apostle	30 November
Serbia	Sava	14 January
Slovakia	Our Lady of Sorrows	15 September
Spain	James the Greater	25 July
Sri Lanka	Lawrence	10 August
Sudan	Josephine Bakhita	8 February
Sweden	Bridget of Sweden	23 July
Switzerland	Gall	16 Octobe
Syria	Barbara	4 December
Ukraine	Josaphat	12 November
USA	Immaculate Conception of Mary	8 December
Wales	David	1 March
West Indies	Rose of Lima	23 August

CURIOUS SAINTLY DEEDS
– PART ONE

- St Antony of Padua once preached to fishes in the Italian town of Rimini because he was so disheartened by the stubborn hearts of the local people.

- In 1884, Pope Leo XIII claimed to have heard a conversation between the Lord and the Devil. He wrote this prayer to St Michael the Archangel after this experience: 'St Michael the Archangel, defend us in the day of battle, be our safeguard against the wickedness and snares of the Devil. May God rebuke him, we humbly pray, and do you the Prince of the Heavenly Host, by the power of God cast into hell Satan and all the other evil spirits, who prowl throughout the world, seeking the ruination of men, Amen.'

- When Attila the Hun was about to invade Paris, St Geneviève urged the townspeople to fast, repent and pray. The threatened invasion never took place.

- On 26 December 1944 (the feast day of the first martyr, St Stephen), Karl Leisner, a Catholic priest, celebrated Mass in a Nazi concentration camp in defiance of the authorities. Shortly afterwards, he was executed. In 1996, he was made a saint.

- St Fabian inadvertently became Pope for 16 years when he wandered into a papal election meeting. A dove descended on his head and the Council took this to be a divine sign that Fabian should be Pope.

- In order to distract himself from impure thoughts at a local dance, St Wulfstan threw himself into a thicket of thorns and thistles. He was never bothered with impure thoughts again.

- St Angela Merici was struck with sudden blindness in 1524 in Crete on her way to the Holy Land. She nevertheless insisted on continuing her journey and experienced a sightless pilgrimage. On her return journey, her sight was restored in Crete.

- St Rose of Lima rubbed her face with pepper because she was too good looking.

- St Maria de la Cabeza's head used to be paraded at the head of a procession in Spain during times of drought.

- St John of the Cross died while in prayer in 1591. In 1926, 335 years later, his body was exhumed to be relocated in a special shrine in his honour. It was found to be remarkably preserved, showing little sign of decay. It was even flexible.

JESUS DAY

In 2000, Texas Governor George W. Bush declared 10 June to be officially recognized as Jesus Day. This is his proclamation (from the Texas State Archives):

OFFICIAL MEMORANDUM
STATE OF TEXAS
OFFICE OF THE GOVERNOR

Throughout the world, people of all religions recognize Jesus Christ as an example of love, compassion, sacrifice and service. Reaching out to the poor, the suffering and the marginalized, he provided moral leadership that continues to inspire countless men, women and children today.

To honor his life and teachings, Christians of all races and denominations have joined together to designate June 10 as Jesus Day. As part of this celebration of unity, they are taking part in the 10th annual March for Jesus in cities throughout the Lone Star State. The march, which began in Austin in 1991, is now held in nearly 180 countries. Jesus Day challenges people to follow Christ's example by performing good works in their communities and neighborhoods. By nursing the sick, feeding the poor or volunteering in homeless shelters, everyone can play a role in making the world a better place.

I urge all Texans to answer the call to serve those in need. By volunteering their time, energy or resources to helping others, adults and youngsters follow Christ's message of love and service in thought and in deed.

Therefore, I, George W. Bush, Governor of Texas, do hereby proclaim June 10 2000

JESUS DAY

Jesus Day takes place each year on the Saturday before Pentecost Sunday, hence the date is not fixed. In 2005, Jesus Day was on 14 May with the theme, 'Created to Love, Called to Serve'.

HYPERDULIA

The Virgin Mary is the most venerated saint and there are numerous forms of piety towards the Mother of God. The term *hyperdulia* refers to the special reverence of Mary. It is the second highest form of reverence permitted in the Catholic Church. *Latria* is the highest reverence, reserved for God alone, and below *hyperdulia* is *dulia*, which is reverence for all the heavenly host.

DE-CANONIZED SAINTS

From the 1960s onwards, after Vatican II, the Catholic Church 'de-canonized' some saints because of lack of evidence about their lives (whether they even existed) and their deeds (whether they performed miracles). Examples of de-canonization include:

- *St Barbara* – possibly an apocryphal saint of either Greek, Italian or Egyptian birth! The dates surrounding her life are uncertain and, as a result of lack of information, she was de-canonized in 1969.

- *Simon of Trent* was canonized in the thirteenth century, but de-canonized in 1965 because of lack of evidence.

- *St Brigit* was de-canonized because she was originally thought to be a pagan goddess, worshipped by the Celts at Kildare in the thirteenth century.

There is some dispute about whether the popular saints, Christopher, Valentine, George, Philomena and Thomas Beckett, are still official saints or whether they have been de-canonized because of the greater number of legendary tales about their lives.

THE WORLD'S WORST DICTATORS

Dictator-watcher David Wallechinsky, in collaboration with Amnesty International, Freedom House, Human Rights Watch and Reporters Without Borders, compiled the following list of the world's worst dictators (2003).

Country	Dictator	Comments
North Korea	1 Kim Jong II	In power since 1994, aka 'The Beloved Leader'.
Burma	2 Than Shwe	Sole leader of military dictatorship since 1991.

China	3 Hu Jintao	China executes more people than the rest of the world put together.
Zimbabwe	4 Robert Mugabe	More than 70,000 people have been killed, tortured or displaced by his regime.
Saudi Arabia	5 Prince Abdullah	More than 8 million foreigners suffer 'slavery-like' conditions.
Equatorial Guinea	6 Teodoro Nguema	More than half the population survive on 60p a day.
Sudan	7 Omar Al Bashir	2 million killed and 4 million homeless from the 20-year civil war.
Turkmenistan	8 Saparmurat Niyazov	Beards, gold teeth and circuses banned. Months of the year named after his mother.
Cuba	9 Fidel Castro	Longest surviving dictator.
Swaziland	10 King Mswati III	Some 300,000 drought-stricken farmers left to suffer starvation.

BLESSING THE THROAT

In many Roman Catholic churches, the lovely ceremony of Blessing the Throat is performed on St Blaise's Day – 3 February. Two long candles are blessed and lit in the form of a St Andrew's Cross. Sufferers from throat ailments kneel while the ribboned cross is laid under their chins and their throats are gently stroked with the ends of the candles. As the candles touch the sufferers, the priest says to each in turn, 'May the Lord deliver you from the evil of the throat, and from every other evil.'

This ceremony derives from the life of St Blaise who was Bishop of Sebaste in Armenia. The most popular account of this Saint – *The Acts of St Blaise* – place his martyrdom in the reign of the Emperor Licinius, around 316. Before becoming a bishop, Blaise may have been a physician and it is thought that he, under divine command, fled to the Armenian mountains to escape Licinius' persecution of Christians.

St Blaise lived for some time in caves with wild animals that he blessed and healed as the need arose. He is reputed to have rescued a pig from a wolf's fangs and restored it. For these actions, he is known as one of the patron saints of wild animals.

His most famous healing took place on his way to trial. A child who had swallowed a fish bone was about to die through choking. St Blaise touched the child's throat and dislodged the bone, thus saving the child's life. For centuries after this act, St Blaise has been invoked for every kind of throat ailment. It was common for country priests to remove throat obstructions by holding the sufferer in both hands and saying, 'Blaise, the martyr and servant of Jesus Christ, commands thee to pass up and down'.

Interestingly, because of the manner of his torture before martyrdom (his skin was torn with sharp iron combs), Blaise is also the patron saint of wool combers. His feast day throughout Britain during the nineteenth century was an occasion for great processions involving everyone from the wool trades.

An extract from a report in the *Leeds Mercury* of 5 February 1825 shows the scale of the celebration in Bradford, a major wool industry town:

> The different trades began to assemble at eight o'clock in the morning, but it was near ten o'clock before they all were arranged in marching order in Westgate. The arrangements were actively superintended by Matthew Thompson, Esq.

The morning was brilliantly beautiful. As early as seven o'clock, strangers poured into Bradford from the surrounding towns and villages, in such numbers as to line the roads in every direction; and almost all the vehicles within twenty miles were in requisition. Bradford was never before known to be so crowded with strangers. Many thousands of individuals must have come to witness the scene. About ten o'clock the procession was drawn up in the following order:—

Herald bearing a flag.
Woolstaplers on horseback, each horse
caparisoned with a fleece.
Worsted Spinners and Manufacturers on
horseback, in white stuff waistcoats, with
each a sliver over the shoulder, and
a white stuff sash; the horses'
necks covered with nets
made of thick yarn.
Merchants on horseback, with coloured
sashes.
Three Guards, Masters' Colours, Three Guards.
Apprentices and Masters' Sons, on horseback,
with ornamented caps, scarlet stuff
coats, white stuff waistcoats, and
blue pantaloons.
Bradford and *Keighley Bands.*
Mace-bearer, on foot.
Six Guards. KING. QUEEN. Six Guards.
Guards. JASON. PRINCESS MEDEA. Guards.
Bishop's Chaplain.
BISHOP BLAISE.
Shepherd and Shepherdess.
Shepherd Swains.
Woolsorters, on horseback, with ornamented
caps, and various coloured slivers.
Comb Makers.
Charcoal Burners.

Combers' Colours.
Band.
Woolcombers, with wool wigs, &c.
Band.
Dyers, with red cockades, blue aprons, and
crossed slivers of red and blue.

ST JEROME AND THE LION

St Jerome lived during the third century and is one of the four Latin Fathers of the Church. He was born into a wealthy family and is the patron saint of scholars and librarians. A brilliant intellectual, who possessed one of the world's greatest libraries, he lived a pagan life until his baptism around the age of 30.

He diligently studied the life of Christ, but felt his love of non-Christian works would lead him astray. So he became a hermit in Arabia, put on sackcloth, and lived a life of prayer and fasting until he became quite emaciated. His love of learning and desire to know his Saviour led to his studying the Scriptures in Hebrew. Although he struggled with the language, he eventually mastered it and today he is renowned for giving us the first accurate Latin translation of the Bible.

Eventually, he retired to Bethlehem and lived in a monastery that he founded. A lovely story relates that while he was in Bethlehem he saw a lion limping as if in pain. The lion approached him and, while others fled in terror, Jerome took the lion's paw and extracted a thorn. From that time on, the grateful lion refused to leave the saint and Jerome used it to bring him wood from a nearby forest.

The last part of Jerome's life in Bethlehem was full of trouble. From all parts of the Roman Empire news came of the invasion of the barbarians, and in 410 the Goths, under Alaric, sacked Rome itself. Like other countries, the north of Palestine was laid waste, and the monks had to share their scanty food with the crowd that poured into the monasteries for refuge. Tradition holds that St Jerome died in 420 in Bethlehem, with his head resting in the manger where Our Lord was born.

Travellers to Bethlehem are still led through a passage cut in the rock to the cell where Jerome wrote his commentaries, epistles and translations, which have given him a foremost place among students of the Bible.

BOND VILLAINS

The fate of a James Bond villain is nearly always clear cut; by the final scenes, he (for most of them are male) is to die in a gruesome manner. The list of Bond villains and their fate are as follows:

Film	Villain	Fate
Dr No	Dr Julius No	Thrown into a pool of toxic waste by Bond.
From Russia With Love	Rosa Klebb	Killed by Tatiana in the final scene.
Goldfinger	Auric Goldfinger	Sucked out of the cabin of an aeroplane.
Thunderball	Emilio Largo	Speared in the back by Domino.

You Only Live Twice	Ernst Blofeld	Escaped on a monorail.
On Her Majesty's Secret Service	Ernst Blofeld	Presumed dead after a car chase.
Diamonds are Forever	Ernst Blofeld	Presumed dead after falling into the ocean.
Live and Let Die	Dr Kananga	Blown up by a pressurized bullet.
The Man with the Golden Gun	Francisco Scaramanga	Shot by Bond.
The Spy Who Loved Me	Karl Stromberg	Shot by Bond.
Moonraker	Hugo Drax	Shot by Bond.
For Your Eyes Only	Aris Kristatos	Shot by Columbo.
Octopussy	Kamal Khan	Flew into a cliff face.
A View to a Kill	Max Zorin	Airship blew up.
The Living Daylights	Georgi Koskov	Arrested and put in prison.
Licence to Kill	Franz Sanchez	Shot by Bond.
Goldeneye	Alec Trevelyan (006)	Impaled on a pole by Bond.
Tomorrow Never Dies	Elliott Carver	Destroyed by his own torpedo.
The World Is Not Enough	Renard	Speared by a nuclear fuel rod.
Die Another Day	Gustav Graves	Chopped up by a jet engine.

IF THOU WILT BE PERFECT . . .

Peter Waldo (1140–1218) was a rich merchant of Lyons, France. One day, he asked a priest how he could live like Jesus Christ. The priest quoted the words of Jesus to the rich young ruler, 'If thou wilt be perfect, go and sell that thou hast, and give it to the poor, and thou shalt have treasure in heaven: and come and follow me' (Matthew 19. 21). Waldo made financial provision for his wife, put his daughters in a convent, and gave the rest of his money to the poor. Waldo memorized portions of the Bible, and began preaching to people. As he gained followers, he sent them out in pairs to preach.

Waldo's followers called themselves 'the Poor in Spirit'. They were also known as the 'Poor of Lyons', the Waldensians (after Waldo), the Wandenses (a variation of Waldensians), and the Vaudois (Vaudes is French for Waldo). The Waldensians were orthodox in their beliefs, but they were outside of the organizational structure of the Roman Catholic Church.

They travelled in pairs, preaching the gospel. They were humble people who believed in 'apostolic poverty'. Travelling barefoot, owning nothing, and sharing all things in common.

The humility and voluntary poverty of the Waldensians were a striking contrast to the pride and luxury of the hierarchy of the Roman Catholic Church. For example, Pope Innocent III (who reigned from 1198 to 1216) wore clothes covered with gold and jewels. He made kings and cardinals kiss his foot. He said that the Pope is 'less than God but more than man'.

Waldo's beliefs were founded on the Bible, especially the Gospels. He believed that there was no need to interpret the Bible because it spoke clearly for itself. All that was needed was to make the whole of Scripture available to the people. Waldo was French, so he commissioned two priests to translate the Bible into French, starting with the Gospels. As soon as the first Gospel had been translated, Waldo applied it to his life 'to the letter' and began preaching it to the people.

Waldo and his followers were excommunicated by Pope Lucius III in 1184 after they refused to stop preaching. Thus began centuries of persecution for a movement that demonstrated the powerful effects of living in accordance with the principles in the Bible. Persecution drove the Waldensians underground in countries such as Italy, Switzerland and Austria. They survived until the sixteenth century, then embraced the Protestant Reformation.

SAINTS AND AMERICAN PLACE NAMES

The history of the United States is reflected in its place names, and there are many saints' names across the 50 American states, including:

County	State	Population	Capital
Saint Bernard	Louisiana	67,229	Chalmette
Saint Charles	Louisiana	48,072	Hahnville
Saint Charles	Missouri	283,883	Saint Charles
Saint Clair	Alabama	64,742	Asheville, Pell City
Saint Clair	Illinois	256,082	Belleville
Saint Clair	Michigan	164,235	Port Huron
Saint Clair	Missouri	9,652	Osceola
Sainte Geneviève	Missouri	17,842	Sainte Geneviève
Saint Francis	Missouri	29,329	Forrest City
Saint Francois	Missouri	55,641	Farmington

Saint Helena	Louisiana	10,525	Greensburg
Saint James	Louisiana	21,216	Convent
Saint Johns	Florida	123,135	Saint Augustine
Saint John the Baptist	Louisiana	43,044	Edgard
Saint Joseph	Indiana	265,559	South Bend
Saint Joseph	Michigan	62,422	Centreville
Saint Landry	Louisiana	87,700	Opelousas
Saint Lawrence	New York	111,931	Canton
Saint Louis	Minnesota	200,528	Duluth
Saint Louis	Missouri	1,016,315	Clayton
Saint Louis	Missouri	348,189	Saint Louis
Saint Lucie	Florida	192,695	Fort Pierce
Saint Martin	Louisiana	48,583	Saint Martinville
Saint Mary	Louisiana	53,500	Franklin
Saint Mary's	Maryland	86,211	Leonardstown
Saint Tammany	Louisiana	191,268	Covington
San Augustine	Texas	8,946	San Augustine
San Benito	California	53,234	Hollister
San Bernardino	California	1,709,434	San Bernardino
San Diego	California	2,813,833	San Diego
San Francisco	California	776,733	San Francisco
San Jacinto	Texas	22,246	Coldspring
San Joaquin	California	563,598	Stockton
San Juan	Colorado	558	Silverton

San Juan	New Mexico	113,801	Aztec
San Juan	Utah	14,413	Monticello
San Juan	Washington	14,077	Friday Harbor
San Luis Obispo	California	246,681	San Luis Obispo
San Mateo	California	707,161	Redwood City
San Miguel	Colorado	6,594	Telluride
San Miguel	New Mexico	30,126	Las Vegas
San Patrico	Texas	67,138	Sinton
San Saba	Texas	6,186	San Saba
Santa Barbara	California	399,347	Santa Barbara
Santa Clara	California	1,682,585	San Jose
Santa Cruz	Arizona	38,381	Nogales
Santa Cruz	California	255,602	Santa Cruz
Santa Fe	New Mexico	129,292	Santa Fe
Santa Rosa	Florida	117,743	Milton

HERESY

One of the primary concerns of early Christianity was that of heresy, generally defined as a departure from traditional Christian beliefs and the creation of new ideas, rituals and forms of worship within the Christian Church. Throughout the ages, Christianity has been buffeted by various heresies, including:

Gnosticism

Followers of this heresy mixed Greek philosophy and Eastern myths with Christianity. They held that God, because he was only good, could not have created a world that contained evil. Therefore, in their view, other forces (or children of God) created our world. One such child was Jesus Christ who came to Earth to share his secret knowledge.

The greatest challenge to traditional Christianity posed by Gnosticism was by Marcion (AD 100–60), who was expelled from the Church for this teaching. After the year 138, his followers formed themselves into a separate body (the Marcionites), though they are also known as the *first Dissenters*. Gnosticism survived long into the Middle Ages, and echoes of it are still to be heard in the teachings of the current-day theosophical movement. (Marcionism survived until about the fifth century AD.)

Montanism

Montanus led this heresy from Phrygia in Turkey in AD 156. The followers of this school of thought were 'zealous, but without knowledge'. For instance, they discouraged marriage, invited martyrdom and set down harsh regimes of fasting. They believed in the imminent end of the world and Christ's immediate return.

When suppression came, the Montanists of Constantinople committed suicide rather than surrender. They gathered in their churches and then set light to them, perishing in the flames.

Monarchianism

This heresy is generally understood to have been responsible for the subsequent rise of another (greater) heresy – Arianism. Followers denied the divinity of Christ, believing him to be an ordinary man who had divine power. For example, Paul of

Samosata, the Bishop of Antioch AD 260–72, preached that Jesus was an ordinary man.

Another branch of this sect disputed the nature of the Trinity.

Arianism

Arius was a priest in Alexandria, who eventually created a storm that would rock the very fundament of Christendom. He protested that his bishop, Alexander of Alexandria, was a monarchian. The subsequent quarrel divided the Church between those who taught that Christ and God were the same and those who taught that God was pre-eminent. Both sides claimed the other as being heretic.

Arius was condemned and excommunicated by a council of over 100 bishops, but another church council threatened to reinstate him. Eventually, Emperor Constantine called on the famous Council of Nicaea – where no less than 300 bishops, together with hundreds of other clergy, were gathered – to decide this problem. Constantine first overruled the Arians, but then changed his mind. So in AD 327 Arius was reinstated and became one of Constantine's advisers.

However, the controversy continued and it required the Eastern Emperor Theodosius to bring together another church council in Constantinople in AD 381. This time the Arians were defeated and the Nicene Creed was officially adopted as the statement of belief for the Christian faith. But it wasn't until the eighth century that Arianism finally disappeared.

Apollinarianism

Apollinaris, Bishop of Laodicea, from about AD 360 began to propagate his idea that Christ had no human soul or spirit, but a divine one. It was an attempt by Apollinaris to reason that Jesus was free of sin, purely divine. This led to a series of edicts by church councils that condemned Apollinarianism as heresy.

Nestorianism

Nestorianus, a monk from Antioch, claimed that Jesus was host to two separate persons – that of the son of God and that of a mortal man. It was, as such, a direct response to Apollinarianism.

Also, Nestorianus, in an attempt to dispel Arianism, disputed the description of 'Mother of God' for Mary – namely because this title indicated that, if Christ was born of her, he had to be younger than her. As he was eternal as God, Mary could only be the mother of Jesus the man.

Scattered remnants of Nestorianism survive today in Iraq, Iran, the United States and South India.

Eutychianism (Monophysitism)

Eutyches was the head of a large monastery near Constantinople and had good contacts at court. His heresy arose as he openly disagreed with the definition of the Christian creed of AD 433 in its condemnation of Nestorianism. He believed that it was a compromise with that heresy, and hence that the Church was guilty of Nestorianism itself.

He claimed that Christ did not possess two natures (divine and human), but that Christ was *of* two natures. In his view, Christ had merged the two natures into one. In AD 451 the great Council of Chalcedon condemned Apollinarianism, Nestorianism and Eutychianism.

Pelagianism

Pelagius, a monk from Britain, gave rise to this heresy. He believed that every child was born absolutely innocent, free of what the traditional Church called 'original sin'. In effect, this meant that Christ was not a saviour who took Adam's original sin upon himself, but merely a teacher who gave mankind an example of what man should be.

Pelagianism is still with us today. Most Christian parents

would struggle to see their new born infant as anything but innocent, and few of them would think they did not possess free will.

SPORTING SAINTS

Team	Sport	Country
New Orleans Saints	American Football	USA
Southampton ('Saints')	Football	England
St Kilda	Aussie Rules Football	Australia
Northampton Saints	Rugby	England
St Helens	Rugby League	England
St Louis Rams	American Football	USA
St Paul Saints	Baseball	USA
St Johnstone	Football	Scotland
St Mirren	Football	Scotland
St Patrick's Athletic	Gaelic football	Eire
St Louis Cardinals	Baseball	USA
St Louis Blues	Ice Hockey	USA

MARY, THE MOTHER OF JESUS

Titles for Mary
Holy Mary,
Holy Mother of God,
Most honoured of virgins,
Chosen daughter of the Father,
Mother of Christ,
Glory of the Holy Spirit
Virgin daughter of Zion,
Virgin poor and humble,
Virgin gentle and obedient,
Handmaid of the Lord,
Mother of the Lord,
Helper of the Redeemed,
Full of grace,
Fountain of beauty,
Model of virtue,
Finest fruit of the redemption,
Perfect disciple of Christ,
Untarnished image of the Church,
Woman transformed,
Woman clothed with the sun,
Woman crowned with stars,
Gentile Lady,
Gracious Lady,
Our Lady,
Joy of Israel,
Splendour of the Church,
Pride of the human race,
Advocate of grace,
Minister of holiness,
Champion of God's people,
Queen of love,
Queen of mercy,
Queen of peace,
Queen of angels,

[53]

Queen of patriarchs and prophets,
Queen of apostles and martyrs,
Queen of confessors and virgins,
Queen of all saints,
Queen conceived without original sin,
Queen assumed into heaven,
Queen of all earth,
Queen of heaven,
Queen of the universe

ST BERNARD DOGS

Around AD 1050, an Augustine monastery was founded along the pass between the Swiss Entremont and the Italian Buthier valleys at 2,438 metres (8,000 feet), in memory of St Bernard, a deacon from Aosta in Italy. Bernard was famous for guarding the mountain pass, thus enabling pilgrims to make their way to and from the holy sites in Rome. The area was notorious for thieves and vagabonds and Bernard helped to make it safe.

It was in the sixteenth century that the pass and the monastery were given the name of St Bernard in recognition of their protective duties. Tibetan mastiffs were used for this purpose and the history of the St Bernard dog is linked with development of the monastery as a safe haven for travellers. Dogs at the monastery (and subsquently the famous hospice) did not live to a great age because the humidity of the area led to them suffering from rheumatism.

Records show that by 1750 mountain guides (or *marroniers*) were routinely accompanied by St Bernard dogs. The dogs' broad chests helped to clear the paths for the travellers. The reports about the dogs' rescue work grew more numerous as it became clear that fatal accidents were decreasing in number. The dogs' primary purpose was to accompany the *marroniers*, as they had an excellent sense of direction. They also possessed an uncanny ability to manoeuvre through heavy fog or snow-storms. The dogs were always accompanied by a monk or *marronier*. However, later on they were allowed on go on rescue missions unaccompanied.

During the 200 or so years that the dogs served on the St Bernard Pass, approximately 2,000 people were rescued. When Napoleon and his army crossed the Alps in May 1800, around 250,000 soldiers travelled through the Pass. The *marroniers* and their dogs were so well organized that, between 1790 and 1810, not one soldier lost his life in the freezing cold of the mountains. The last documented rescue was in 1897 – a 12-year-old boy was found almost frozen to death in a crevice and was awakened by a dog.

The legendary barrel strapped beneath the neck of the dogs, however, seems to have been invented by the famous alpinist Meissner, who wrote in 1816: 'Often the dogs receive a little barrel around their neck with alcoholic beverages and a basket with bread.' The chroniclers from the Hospice never mentioned a barrel. In 1800, however, Canonicus Murith mentioned a little saddle with which the dogs carried milk and butter from the dairy in La Pierre up to the Hospice.

Today, the hospice has 18 St Bernard dogs, but their future is uncertain because instead of these canine helpers of some 60 kilograms, helicopters and heat-seeking equipment are frequently used to rescue people in avalanches.

THE HARP OF THE HOLY SPIRIT

Ephrem (or Ephraim) of Edessa was a teacher, poet, orator, and defender of the faith who died during a famine in AD 373. Edessa was a city in Syria, not far from Antioch – an early centre for the spread of Christian teaching in the East. It is said that in 325 Ephrem accompanied his bishop, James of Nisibis, to the Council of Nicea. His writings are an eloquent defence of the Nicene faith in the deity of Jesus Christ. He countered the Gnostics' practice of spreading their message through popular songs by composing Christian songs and hymns of his own, with great effect. He is known to the Syrian church as 'the harp of the Holy Spirit'. We know of more than 70 of his hymns, numerous Bible commentaries and sermons.

This is one of his well-known poems about fasting, still uttered today in Syria:

O Lord and Master of my life, do not give me the spirit of laziness, meddling, self-importance and idle talk. *[prostration]*

Instead, grace me, Your servant, with the spirit of modesty, humility, patience, and love. *[prostration]*

Indeed, my Lord and King, grant that I may see my own faults,
And not condemn my brothers and sisters, for You are blessed unto ages of ages. Amen. *[prostration]*

[Twelve deep bows, saying each time: 'O God, be gracious to me, a sinner.']

ATHANASIUS OF ALEXANDRIA

Athanasius is revered as a saint by the Roman Catholic and Orthodox denominations, for his outstanding defence of Christianity against the heresy of Arius. Around AD 319, Arius, a church leader, began preaching that Jesus Christ was begotten by God, thus denying the eternality of the Son of God. Athanasius resisted this departure from the Scriptures for most of his life. Although he became Bishop of Alexandria in 318, he was banished at least five times from that city as Arianism took root. It is from his battles with this pernicious heresy that the phrase *Athanasius contra mundum*

(Athanasius against the world) became popular in the fourth century. When he was finally restored to Alexandria, Athanasius formulated a creed that is still recited today to express the unity of the Godhead.

Athanasius was also the first person to identify all 27 books of the New Testament, and his list was accepted by church councils, giving us our New Testament today.

An extract from the Athanasian Creed:

> Whosoever will be saved, before all things it is necessary that he hold the catholic faith;
> Which faith except every one do keep whole and undefiled, without doubt he shall perish everlastingly.
> And the catholic faith is this: That we worship one God in Trinity, and Trinity in Unity;
> Neither confounding the persons nor dividing the substance.
> For there is one person of the Father, another of the Son, and another of the Holy Spirit.
> But the Godhead of the Father, of the Son, and of the Holy Spirit is all one, the glory equal, the majesty coeternal.
> Such as the Father is, such is the Son, and such is the Holy Spirit.
> The Father uncreated, the Son uncreated, and the Holy Spirit uncreated.
> The Father incomprehensible, the Son incomprehensible, and the Holy Spirit incomprehensible.
> The Father eternal, the Son eternal, and the Holy Spirit eternal.
> And yet they are not three eternals but one eternal.

CURIOUS SAINTLY DEEDS
– PART TWO

- St Benno, twelfth-century Bishop of Meissen in Saxony, refused Henry IV (who had been excommunicated) entrance to the Cathedral of Meissen by locking the doors and throwing the key into the River Elbe. He then withdrew to Rome. When he returned to Meissen many months later, he commanded a local fisherman to cast his net into the river. The fisherman brought up a fish with the lost key in its mouth.

- St Cheron, third-century Bishop of Chartres, was on his way to visit St Denis at Paris but was attacked and beheaded by robbers; however, he carried on his journey carrying his head in his hand.

- St Clement is mentioned in Philippians 4.3. He was the third Bishop of Rome and converted many as a result of his miraculous powers. Under the Trajan persecution, Clement was sent with other Christians to work in stone quarries. When they suffered from extreme thirst, Clement prayed and had a vision of Jesus standing near a mountain. Upon digging at this site, a torrent of water was discovered that refreshed them all. Because of this, Clement was thrown into the sea, tied to an anchor. But at the prayer of his brethren, the sea retreated 3 miles.

- St Corentin, the patron saint of Quimper, in Brittany was a fifth-century hermit. Every morning he was sustained by a remarkable fish. Even though Corentin ate a piece of this fish every day, it stayed alive and kept growing. When King Gradlon witnessed this miracle, he had Corentin made the first Bishop of Quimper.

- St Cuthbert was a pupil of St Aidan at Melrose Abbey and later became Bishop of Lindisfarne in the eighth century. He was greatly beloved, and many miracles are attributed to him. On one occasion, he died from long prayers and meditation at the shore, but two otters came out of the water and brought him back to life.

THE LAST SUPPER

Tradition records that in Leonardo da Vinci's masterpiece, 'The Last Supper' the same model was used for the figure of Christ and Judas. The model, Pietro Bandinelli, posed for the portrait of Christ when he was a young chorister in one of Rome's many churches, but for many years da Vinci left the painting unfinished because he could not find the right face to portray Judas. Eventually, he hired a hardened beggar who had hateful features. Da Vinci used him as his model of Judas without realizing he was the same Pietro Bandinelli who years before had looked so much like Christ. The intervening years of sinful living had so marred his countenance that he changed from his Christ-like face to that of the traitor Judas.

RASPUTIN

The last words of Grigory Yefimovich Rasputin, written to Tsarina Alexandra, on 7 December 1916:

 I write and leave behind me this letter at St Petersburg. I feel that I shall leave life before January 1st. I wish to make known to the Russian people, to Papa, to the Russian Mother and to the children, to the land of Russia, what they must understand. If I am killed by common assassins, and especially by my brothers the Russian peasants, you, Tsar of Russia, have nothing to fear, remain on your throne and govern, and you, Russian Tsar, will have nothing to fear for your children, they will reign for hundreds of years in Russia. But if I am murdered by nobles, their hands will remain soiled with my blood, for twenty-five years they will not wash their hands from my blood. They will leave Russia. Brothers will kill brothers, and they will kill each other and hate each other, and for twenty-five years there will be no nobles in the country. Tsar of the land of Russia, if you hear the sound of the bell which will tell you that Grigory has been killed, you must know this: if it was your relations who have wrought my death then no one of your family, that is to say, none of your children or relations, will remain alive for more than two years. They will be killed by the Russian people . . . I shall be killed. I am no longer among the living. Pray, pray, be strong, think of your blessed family.

On 30 December, Rasputin was killed by two relatives of the Tsar Nicholas II, and 19 months after Rasputin's death the Tsar and his family were murdered by their Bolshevik guards.

FAMOUS PRISONERS

Prisoner	Prison	For
Al 'Scarface' Capone	Alcatraz	Tax evasion
George 'Machine Gun' Kelly	Alcatraz	Kidnapping
Robert 'Birdman' Stroud	Alcatraz	Murder
William Wallace	Tower of London	Treason
Guy Fawkes	Tower of London	Treason
Sir Walter Raleigh	Tower of London	Treason
Rudolph Hess	Tower of London for four days	Prisoner of war
Anne Boleyn	Tower of London	Treason
Catherine Howard	Tower of London	Treason
Lady Jane Grey	Tower of London	Treason
William Penn	Tower of London	Publication of *The Sandy Foundation Shaken*
Nelson Mandela	Robben Island	Inciting people to go on strike
Winston Churchill	Held by the Boers in 1899	Prisoner of war
Vaclav Havel	Imprisoned three times in Czechoslovakia	Political activities
Fidel Castro	Imprisoned by the Cuban government in 1953	Political activities

Mahatma Gandhi	Imprisoned by the British in 1913	Political activities
Eamon De Valera	Imprisoned by the British in 1916	Easter Rising
Fyodor Dostoyevsky	Four years hard labour in Semipalatinsk	Dissent
John Bunyan	Bedford Jail	Refusal to stop preaching
Daniel Defoe	Newgate	Anti-establishment pamphlets
Bertrand Russell	Imprisoned for five months in London in 1918	Libelling the American Army

THE CONVERSION OF A CROOK

No one is too sinful, too wayward or beyond God's mercy. This wonderful truth is attested to by a brief look at the life of a celebrated sinner who became a powerful instrument of God.

Jerry McAuley was an Irishman who in 1852 was sent to live with his sister in New York, at the age of 13. He lived in the Water Street district of that city and soon became notorious for leading a gang of thugs and thieves. Many times he was in trouble with the law, and by the time he was 19 he had been sentenced to 15 years' imprisonment in Sing Sing Prison.

Five years into his sentence, he went to the Sunday chapel service and heard the testimony of Orville 'Awful' Gardiner. Gardiner had been one of McAuley's crime partners, but he could not deny that a great transformation had taken place in

Gardiner's life. McAuley tried many times to pray for a similar conversion, but struggled to know whether God would forgive him.

Eventually, he found that forgiveness and described that moment thus:

> All at once it seemed as if something supernatural was in my room. I was afraid to open my eyes. I was in an agony and the tears rolled off my face in great drops. How I longed for God's mercy! Just then, in the very height of my distress, it seemed as if a hand was laid upon my head and these words came to me: 'My son, thy sins which are many, are forgiven.' I do not know if I heard a voice, yet the words were distinctly spoken in my soul. I jumped from my knees. I paced up and down my cell. A heavenly light seemed to fill it. A softness and a perfume like the fragrance of flowers. I did not know if I was living or not. I clapped my hands and shouted, 'Praise God! Praise God.'

McAuley was released from Sing Sing in 1864 after serving seven years as a result of his reformed life. However, he struggled with being a Christian in the outside world and relapsed several times into crime and drunkenness.

In 1869 McAuley was at the centre of a revival that broke out in the Water Street district. This renewal became known as the John Allen Excitement after the evangelistic preaching of that godly man. McAuley was swept up in this movement and experienced a tremendous spiritual empowering. Fired by the 'Excitement', McAuley and his friend Fredrick Hatch started the 'Helping Hand for Men' mission on 316 Water Street. Night after night they cared for drunks and tramps from the nearby slums. They ministered to thousands of destitute people and preached the gospel to them, as well as taking care of their physical needs.

Although McAuley died in 1884, his influence is still powerful today as there are now hundreds of 'rescue missions', inspired by his example, throughout the United States.

THE 26 MARTYRS OF NAGASAKI

Jesuit missionary Francis Xavier went to Japan in 1549 and succeeded in attracting converts to the Catholic Church. He left after a few years, though, having established several churches and appointed local leaders. Christianity was tolerated in Japan at this time because there was a great interest in developing trading links with the West.

However, the political ruler of Japan (not the Emperor), Toyotomi Hideyoshi, for political reasons began to persecute the few Christians in the country. Believers were arrested, imprisoned and forced to renounce their faith. One of the most notorious incidents took place on 5 February 1597 when 26 men (19 Japanese), among them priests, were forced to march from Osaka to Nagasaki. On the way, their left ears were cut off and they were subjected to cruel tortures. Upon reaching Nagasaki, each man was crucified and then stabbed to death with a spear. None of the men renounced their faith.

As always, this persecution had the opposite effect from what the authorities intended. Instead of snuffing out the faith, the courage of the 26 martyrs inspired other Christians and led to new converts. For a few years, Nagasaki became a major centre of Christianity in the country, as this place of martyrdom was venerated by many pilgrims.

Eventually, in the 1620s, the government expelled all foreigners from Japan. Christianity was absolutely forbidden and contact with the West was broken off, save for a few trading links.

It was not until 250 years later that French priests were allowed back into Japan, and one of their first tasks was to open a church in Nagasaki. They were amazed to discover that native Christians still existed, in spite of the authorities' best attempts to banish them.

Today, there is a monument to the 26 martyrs in Nagasaki at the Martyrs Museum.

FAREWELL, SWEET LIGHT!

St Ambrose, the famed Archbishop of Milan who died in 397, recounts that: 'Theothmus, on being told by his physician that except he did abstain from drink and excess, he was likely to lose his sight. His heart was so desperately set on sin that he said, "Vale lumen amicum: farewell, sweet light! I must have my pleasure in my sin!"'

ANTEPENDIUM

 The antependium or *pallium* was the great veil of silk or precious metal that surrounded a saint's altar in the Middle Ages. It was also placed on the tomb itself as a sign of veneration and respect. For example, the basilica of St Ambrosio at Milan preserves an antependium from the ninth century made of gold and covered with precious stones. Where cloth was used, the antependium was often changed with great ceremony.

FOUR CHAPLAINS

On 3 February 1943, the US ship *Dorchester* was torpedoed by a German U boat. On board were four chaplains from the Army Chaplain Corps. Unlike most of the other sailors, the four chaplains had gone to bed with their lifejackets on. When the torpedo hit, many of the sailors could not find their life-jackets in time. In an act of incredible selflessness, the four chaplains gave their own lifejackets to the other sailors, knowing that by doing so they would go down with the sinking ship. Witnesses testified that they last saw the four chaplains with their arms linked together, praying as the ship sank.

This act of courage was recognized with the award of posthumous medals of heroism and a special stamp, issued in 1948. Today, 3 February is designated by the United States Congress as 'Four Chaplains Day'.

The four chaplains were:

- George L. Fox – Methodist minister
- Alexander D. Goode – Rabbi
- Clark V. Poling – Minister of the Dutch Reformed Church
- John P. Washington – Roman Catholic priest

CURIOUS SAINTLY DEEDS
– PART THREE

- St Paul the Apostle was beheaded outside the Ostian Gate in Rome around AD 65, the same day as the Apostle Peter was martyred inside the city. Tradition records that as Paul's head was struck off, it bounced three times on the ground. At each place where it touched, a fountain of water sprang up – the first one hot, the second one warm, and the third one cold.

- St Marcarius was one of the most famous Egyptian hermits; he died in the fourth century. Many stories are told about him, including the tale of Marcarius finding the skull of an ancient mummy. He asked the skull who it was and it replied 'a pagan'. When the hermit asked where its soul was, the skull replied, 'Deep in hell!'

- St Isidore is the patron saint of farmers. He was a poor, ignorant peasant whose cruel master did not allow him time for his devotions. However, Isidore continued to pray and worship. His master was converted when he saw the saint deep in prayer and two angels ploughing for him!

- St Herman-Joseph has the latter name because he claimed the Virgin Mary so favoured him that one day she appeared to him in a vision, called him her husband, and put a ring upon his finger.

- St Laurence was from Aragon in Spain and martyred in AD 258 in Rome. He received, from the people of Rome, the title 'Il cotese Spagnuolo' – the Courteous Spaniard. This was because when, 200 years after his death, his tomb was opened to deposit the relics of St Stephen, it was discovered he had moved to the left to accommodate him.

- St Martin of Tours was famed for many miracles. It is said that on one occasion, the Emperor Valentinian came to see him, but failed to show him respect by rising from his chair. However, he quickly got up when the chair suddenly burst into flames.

PLACES LINKED WITH ST PATRICK

The much loved St Patrick came to Ireland in AD 432, on a mission from Pope Celestine I to convert the heathen natives. At that time, Ireland was steeped in Druidism, but Patrick performed many miracles and faithfully presented the Christian faith to the Irish. By the time he died in AD 461, much of the country abandoned Druidism and there was a revival throughout the land.

In Ireland, many places are associated with Patrick, including:

Place	Significance
Lough Derg (Lake of the Red Eye)	An island in County Donegal. It was the last stronghold of the Druids and, according to legend, Patrick slew the monster of the lake here which turned the water red.
Ard Macha	Known today as Armagh. Patrick is reputed to have built the Cathedral Church here.
Ceanannas Mór	Contains the remains of a monastery used by Patrick. Monks from this area created the world-famous *Book of Kells* in the ninth century.
Croagh Phádraig	Upon this mountain in Westport, County Mayo, Patrick spent 40 days fasting and praying.
Sabhail	County Down, allegedly the place where Patrick died.
Dun Phadraig	This fortress in Northern Ireland houses the Cathedral Church of the Holy Trinity, the site of Patrick's burial. St Columba is also supposed to be buried here.

JOHANN TETZEL

Johann Tetzel was a sixteenth-century Dominican priest and master seller of indulgences. Armed with papal authority, he would travel from village to village throughout Germany with printed receipts from the Pope guaranteeing release from purgatory into paradise in exchange for money. Indulgences were popular among the poor, but they were the ones least able to afford them. The money was used to make the Vatican look even grander.

Fraudsters like Tetzel led to Martin Luther posting his famous Ninety-five Theses against papal excesses in Wittenberg on 31 October 1517. Sales of indulgences fell considerably after this.

Tetzel was also accused of immorality and he was disowned by the establishment for his over-enthusiastic sales pitch. He died in 1519. On his deathbed, Luther wrote to him about the forgiveness and salvation offered by Jesus.

One of Tetzel's popular sayings was:

When the coin in the coffer rings, the soul from purgatory springs.

TEN FALSE MESSIAHS

There have been many false messiahs throughout the centuries, claiming divinity and special revelation to restore the greatness of Israel. This is a list of some of these failed deliverers:

Name	What they claimed
Simon Bar Kokhba (132)	Revolted against the Romans and proclaimed himself 'a star, arisen out of Jacob' (Numbers 24.17). Beheaded by the Roman General Julius Severus.
Moses of Crete (450)	Claimed to be a second Moses, but failed to part the Aegean Sea for the people to cross to Israel.

David Alroy (1147)	Skilled magician who revolted against the Sultan of Persia.
Abraham Abulafia (1240–91)	Claimed God had anointed him Messiah in Sicily in 1248. Tried to convert Pope Nicholas III to Judaism!
David Reuveni (1490–1538)	Sought Pope Clement VII's support for a Holy Land crusade. Declared a messiah by Spanish and Portuguese Jews.
Isaac Luria (1534–72)	Claimed he was taught by the prophet Elijah. Developed a new form of Kabbalah. Died at the age of 38 during a flu epidemic.
Hayyim Vital (1542–1620)	A disciple of Luria, and claimed that Luria had made him his successor.
Shabbatai Zevi (1626–76)	Rode to Jerusalem on a white horse, circled the city seven times, and claimed to be able to locate the ten lost tribes. Failed to capture Turkey. Eventually converted to Islam.
Jacob Frank (1726–91)	Expelled from Turkey, converted to Islam, but still claimed messiahship. Died as a result of a stroke.
Rebbe Menechem Mendel Schneerson (1902–94)	Proclaimed as the messiah by the Lubavatcher Chassidic movement in New York. Never visited Israel. Died following a stroke in 1994, but still has a large following.

COLONEL THOMAS BLOOD

Thomas Blood was one of history's most daring criminals. During the English Civil War, he was a spy for Cromwell's forces and was rewarded with land in lieu of wages. After the monarchy was restored, he twice tried to kidnap James Butler, the Lord Lieutenant of Ireland, from Dublin Castle in 1663. Both attempts failed and Blood escaped to Holland dressed as a Quaker!

His most famous criminal activity was an attempt to steal the Crown Jewels from the Tower of London in 1671. Over several months, Blood befriended Talbot Edwards, the Keeper of the Crown Jewels. Eventually, he persuaded Edwards to show him (and his accomplices) the famous Jewels. When Blood and his accomplices were let into the Jewel Chamber, Edwards was quickly bound and gagged. Blood and his gang made off with the Crown Jewels, but somehow Edwards managed to sound the alarm. They were all captured before they left the Tower.

Ironically, Blood and his gang were imprisoned in the Tower. Everyone thought they would hang at Tyburn, but Blood insisted on a meeting with the King. The outcome of that meeting, which took place on 18 July 1671, was that although Blood and his gang were guilty of treason, they were pardoned by the King. In addition, Blood was granted a sum of £500 (a great deal of money at that time) a year for the rest of his life. One explanation for this curious turn of events is that Blood may have served King Charles II as a double agent and his crime was thus overlooked. Another explanation is that he persuaded the King that he wanted to sell the Crown Jewels to bring much needed money into the King's treasury.

Blood died in 1680 in London, but such was his reputation for trickery that his remains were exhumed in 1684 to confirm his identity.

CURIOUS SAINTLY DEEDS
– PART FOUR

- St Thomas of Villanueva was made Archbishop of Valencia in the sixteenth century. He was renowned for his service to the poor and frequently gave away clothes and food to help them. On one occasion, his appearance was so poverty-stricken that his chapter presented him with a large sum of money to buy new clothes. But Thomas gave all the money to the hospital. His great example earned him the title 'Thomas the Almoner'.

- St Etheldreda was an East Anglian Saxon princess in the seventh century. She had a dream that her staff became a great tree. She took this to mean that she must establish a place of religious learning, and so founded Ely Cathedral and monastery, becoming its first abbess. Four hundred years after she died, St Etheldreda is said to have visited and released a repentant sinner who was about to be hanged for his crimes. The man vowed to serve God in the monastery of Ely.

- Clovis, King of the Franks in the sixth century, had a faithful wife, St Clotilda. However, Clovis was not a believer, despite his wife's earnest prayers which seemed to be in vain. But one day on the battlefield Clovis was facing defeat, and called on Clotilda's God and was saved. He emerged victorious from the battle and was baptized by St Remi. At his baptism, tradition holds that a vial of oil came miraculously down from heaven, together with three lilies for Clovis, Clotilda and Remi. Thus the banner of France was changed from three toads to the fleur-de-lys.

- St Ambrose, one of the four Latin fathers of the Church, is the patron saint of Milan. As an infant, a swarm of bees is said to have gathered around his mouth without hurting him, signifying his future eloquence. Many miracles are

attributed to Ambrose. For example, when the Cathedral of Milan was being consecrated, he had a vision that showed him where the relics of St Gervasius and St Protasius were. Once, when he was preaching, he saw an angel encouraging him and he had a vision of the burial of St Martin of Tours taking place in France.

- St Eloy is the patron saint of all metal workers. He was Master of the Mint in Bologna in the seventh century and made many sacred objects for his church. It is said that on many occasions Eloy was tormented by a demon while using his metal-working skills. On one occasion, like St Dunstan, Eloy seized the demon by the nose with his red hot pincers and it fled. Another time, a demon-possessed horse was brought to him that refused to be shod. Eloy cut off the horse's leg, put on the shoe, and replaced the leg by making the sign of the cross.

FIFTH MONARCHY

In Cromwellian England, a Puritan sect known as the Fifth Monarchy Men arose in 1649. They were thus called because they believed they were the successors to the preceding four major monarchies – the Assyrian, the Persian, the Greek and the Roman. They sought to establish a millennial reign of Christ on earth and aimed to abolish all existing laws and the established order. This was to be replaced by Mosaic laws. They had high hopes that Oliver Cromwell would establish such a 'new world order', but they were disappointed when the Protector failed to meet their demands. The Fifth Monarchy Men leaders Christopher Feake and John Rogers were arrested in 1661 and the movement gradually died out – although seeds of it remained for over 100 years.

THE HEAD OF JOHN
THE BAPTIST

On Herod's birthday the daughter of Herodias danced for them and pleased Herod so much that he promised with an oath to give her whatever she asked. Prompted by her mother, she said, 'Give me here on a platter the head of John the Baptist.' The king was distressed, but because of his oaths and his dinner guests, he ordered that her request be granted and had John beheaded in the prison. His head was brought in on a platter and given to the girl, who carried it to her mother.

Mark 14. 6–12

The head of St John the Baptist, the precursor of Christ, has many stories related to it. For instance, the Russian Orthodox Church believes that this famous relic was found and lost at least three times. On the final occasion the head was found (uncorrupted) in 823 in 'the bowels of the earth' where it had been specially hidden by angels. It was transferred from the city of Comana (near the Black Sea) to Constantinople. This find is commemorated by this denomination on 25 May every year as a Third Class Feast.

CURIOUS RUSSIAN SAINTS

- St Andrew became known as the 'Fool for Christ' because he believed he had a calling to act as if insane. He was thrown out of Constantinople and became a beggar. However, his fellow beggars could not stand his behaviour and shunned him. His madness enabled him to pray for those who hurt him and retain his great humility. He is thought to have died in AD 936, aged 66.

- St Herman is reckoned to be the first 'American' Saint of the Russian Orthodox Church. He came to Alaska as a young monk in 1794 and practised an asceticism so severe that no one knew what it was! However, a part of his calling was to carry heavy chains (weighing around 10 kilograms), use two bricks instead of a pillow, and eat very little.

- St Seraphim (Vasyly Nikolaevich Mooraviev), towards the end of his life – in 1940 – prayed for 1,000 days for the salvation of Russia while standing on a rock. It is said that his intercession saved Russia from the Nazis.

- St Agapit was the first recognized medical doctor in Kiev, in the eleventh century. He was also a revered monk who performed many healings, and combined prayers with more conventional techniques such as using herbs. He never accepted payment and was known to have cured many conditions, including leprosy.

COUNT ALESSANDRO DI CAGLIOSTRO

Infamous charlatan, magician and adventurer who enjoyed enormous success in Parisian high society in the years preceding the French Revolution. Born Guiseppe Balsamo in

1743, he took the more impressive-sounding name (and title) Count Alessandro di Cagliostro and travelled throughout Europe posing as an alchemist (selling elixirs of youth and love powders), soothsayer, medium and miraculous healer. By 1785, his séances were gripping Parisian fashionable society.

However, his luck came to an end in 1789 when he was arrested in Rome. His wife had denounced him to the Inquisition as a heretic, magician, conjuror and Freemason. After his trial he was sentenced to death, but this was later commuted to life imprisonment in the fortress of San Leo in the Apennines where he died in 1795.

ST PONTIUS PILATE

Strange but true – Pontius Pilate, fifth governor of Judea from AD 26, is considered a saint, along with his wife Claudia Procula, by the Abyssinian Church. Their tradition holds that Pilate repented of his death sentence upon Jesus after his wife converted him. The acceptance of her Christian faith goes back to the second century; it was believed by no less an authority than Origen. The date of 25 June is assigned to St Pontius and St Procula in the Abyssinian Church and the Greek Church assigns 27 October as a feast day for St Procula.

THE RIGHTEOUS AND THE WICKED COMPARED IN PROVERBS 10

- *Proverbs 10. 3* – The LORD does not let the righteous go hungry, but he thwarts the craving of the wicked.

- *Proverbs 10. 6* – Blessings crown the head of the righteous, but violence overwhelms the mouth of the wicked.

- *Proverbs 10. 7* – The memory of the righteous will be a blessing, but the name of the wicked will rot.

- *Proverbs 10. 8* – The wise in heart accept commands, but a chattering fool comes to ruin.

- *Proverbs 10. 9* – The man of integrity walks securely, but he who takes crooked paths will be found out.

- *Proverbs 10. 11* – The mouth of the righteous is a fountain of life, but violence overwhelms the mouth of the wicked.

- *Proverbs 10. 14* – Wise men store up knowledge, but the mouth of a fool invites ruin.

- *Proverbs 10. 16* – The wages of the righteous bring them life, but the income of the wicked brings them punishment.

- *Proverbs 10. 20* – The tongue of the righteous is choice silver, but the heart of the wicked is of little value.

- *Proverbs 10. 21* – The lips of the righteous nourish many, but fools die for lack of judgment.

- *Proverbs 10. 27* – The fear of the LORD adds length to life, but the years of the wicked are cut short.

- *Proverbs 10. 28* – The prospect of the righteous is joy, but the hopes of the wicked come to nothing.

GOOD KING WENCESLAS

This well-known 'king' was actually the Duke of Bohemia (part of the Czech Republic). He was born in 907. Wenceslas's father, Wratislaw, was a Christian but his mother was pagan. He was raised by his grandmother, Ludmilla, who was also a Christian.

Wenceslas became Duke in 922 and sought to christianize the Bohemians. He was keen to introduce the Benedictine Order into his kingdom and was noted for his piety and good works among the poor. Many miracles are associated with Wenceslas. For example, when Radislas, the prince of an invading army, sought to slay him, he saw two angels alongside Wenceslas and heard a heavenly voice warning him not to strike the Duke. He was so astonished at these manifestations that he fell at the feet of Wenceslas and begged his pardon.

It is thought that Wenceslas was murdered by his brother, Boleslas, sometime between 922 and 938. The Duke had provided a banquet at his brother's palace. After the banquet he went to pray, as was his custom, and egged on by his mother, Boleslas struck him down with his sword.

Boleslas was overcome with grief by his actions and had the bones of his brother taken to the church of St Vitus in Prague, where they quickly attracted pilgrims. Within 20 years of his death, he was recognized as the patron saint of Bohemia and his feast day (28 September) is still kept in that land.

The popular carol is thought to have originated in the thirteenth century, although its first recorded appearance was in 1582. The words of today's carol were composed by John Neal, and the music is based on a thirteenth-century spring carol:

Good King Wenceslas looked out
On the feast of Stephen
When the snow lay round about
Deep and crisp and even
Brightly shone the moon that night
Though the frost was cruel
When a poor man came in sight
Gath'ring winter fuel

THE BLOOD OF ST GENNARO

The patron saint of Naples, St Gennaro (or Janarius), is reputed to perform a twice yearly miracle – his dried blood is supposed to liquefy and bubble like fresh blood on at least two days: 19 September and on the Saturday before the first Sunday in May. On these days, the authorities from the Cathedral in Naples display a vial of the saint's liquefied blood to the populace and lead a procession through the city streets.

It is thought that Janarius was martyred during the reign of the Emperor Diocletian in 305. His relics were taken to Pozzuoli, Beneventum and then to Naples. The saint's presence is reputed to have stopped the eruptions of Mount Vesuvius and brought about many healings in the city. Local people believe that if the blood fails to liquefy, disasters such as plague, war and earthquakes are imminent. In 1943, there was great consternation when the blood failed to liquefy.

There have been scientific attempts to explain the phenomenon of blood liquefaction, but so many explanations have been offered that it is difficult to know the truth. In addition, it is claimed that the relics of other saints also manifest blood liquefaction in various degrees, including John the Baptist, Stephen and Pantaleone.

[79]

ST POL AND THE DRAGON

In the sixth century, a Welsh prince called Pol became the first Bishop of Leon. He lived in Brittany and had a strange diet that consisted solely of bread and water. He is said to have performed many wonders, including ridding the nearby Isle of Ratz from a terrible dragon by commanding it to cast itself into the sea.

It is said that in Leon Cathedral there still exists Pol's little bell which was found by the saint in the mouth of a fish. This legendary bell is said to cure headaches and similar afflictions by all who listen to it.

THE SIN OF SIMONY

'Disputation with Simon Magus', Fillippino Lippi, 1481.

Simony is the offence of buying or selling for profit something that is spiritual. It is named after Simon Magus, whose story is told in Acts 8. He was a great magician who sought to purchase the power of the Holy Spirit for financial gain.

Now for some time a man named Simon had practised sorcery in the city and amazed all the people of Samaria. He boasted that he was someone great, and all the people, both high and low, gave him their attention and exclaimed, 'This man is the divine power known as the Great Power.' They followed him because he had amazed them for a long time with his magic. But when they believed Philip as he preached the good news of the kingdom of God and the name of Jesus Christ, they were baptized, both men and women. Simon himself believed and was baptised. And he followed Philip everywhere, astonished by the great signs and miracles he saw . . . When Simon saw that the Spirit was given at the laying on of the apostles' hands, he offered them money and said, 'Give me also this ability so that everyone on whom I lay my hands may receive the Holy Spirit' (Acts 8. 9–19).

Simony was prohibited by church councils in the third and fourth centuries. But the practice of using money to buy church offices increased and is mentioned as a sin in Dante's *Inferno*, and by Machiavelli, who called, 'luxury, simony and cruelty as three dear friends and handmaids of the Pope'.

The penalty for simony was the forfeiture of any gain from the transaction.

TOUCHING FOR THE KING'S EVIL

That pious monarch, Edward the Confessor (1003–66), began the tradition of 'touching' or laying hands on his subjects to effect a cure for their ailments. According to the *Chronicles of the Kings of England*, a young woman who suffered from 'humours collecting abundantly about her neck, she had contracted a sore disorder, the glands swelling in a dreadful manner' had a  dream to have the affected area washed by the King. When the lady's neck was washed by Edward, 'the lurid skin opened, so that worms flowed out with the purulent matter, and the tumour subsided; but as the orifice of the ulcer was large and unsightly, he commanded her to be supported at the royal expense till she should be perfectly cured. However, before a week was expired, a fair new skin returned, and hid the ulcers so completely that nothing of the original wound could be discovered.' The disease was probably scrofula and was difficult to heal at that time.

The practice of Touching for the King's Evil prevailed with subsequent monarchs and, in 1683, King Charles II regulated this curious ceremony. From that time, 'Publick Healings' were conducted by the King from All Hallows Eve until a week before Christmas and after Christmas until the first week of March. Each person had to be recommended by their minister and issued with a certificate confirming that the individual had an incurable disease and had not previously been touched for the evil.

Many hundreds of cases were recorded of healings being performed by kings from the time of Edward the Confessor onwards, but no records have been uncovered of people who were not cured. It is probable that the psychological impact of the attention of a royal personage did much to assuage the tumours associated with scrofula, but no scientific evidence has been produced to explain this phenomenon completely.

The Touching for the King's Evil is referred to by Shakespeare in *Macbeth*, King Duncan having been a contemporary of Edward the Confessor:

Macduff.—What's the disease he means?
Malcolm.—'Tis called the evil:
A most miraculous work in this good king;
Which often, since my here-remain in England,
I've seen him do. How he solicits heaven,
Himself best knows: but strangely-visited people,
All swoll'n and ulcerous, pitiful to the eye,
The mere despair of surgery, he cures,
Hanging a golden stamp about their necks,
Put on with holy prayers: and 'tis spoken,
To the succeeding royalty he leaves
The healing benediction

Macbeth, *Act 4, Scene 3*

ST DISTAFF'S DAY

The first free day after the Twelve Days of Christmas is 7 January and takes the name of Distaff Day or Rock Dag because, in ancient times, men and women resumed work after the long holiday – the women to their spinning (using a distaff) and the men to ploughing.

It was a day of work and play because it was difficult to resume work after the long break and many pranks were played. Indolent men set fire to the flax of their womenfolk and they doused the men with pails of water! This popular ritual is captured in Robert Herrick's (1591–1674) poem:

St Distaff's Day; Or, the Morrow after Twelfth-day

> Partly work and partly play
> You must on St Distaffs Day:
> From the plough soon free your team;
> Then cane home and fother them:
> If the maids a-spinning go,
> Burn the flax and fire the tow.
> Bring in pails of water then,
> Let the maids bewash the men.
> Give St Distaff' all the right:
> Then bid Christmas sport good night,
> And next morrow every one
> To his own vocation.

THE VICAR OF BRAY

Simon Aleyn was the renowned Vicar of Bray in Berkshire from 1540 to 1588. His notoriety arises from changing his faith to suit the religion of the reigning monarch. He was a Protestant during the reigns of Henry VIII and Edward VI, became a

Catholic during the reign of Mary, and reverted to being a
Protestant when Elizabeth I became Queen. His resolve to
remain the Vicar of Bray, whatever the circumstances, gave
rise to a famous ballad:

The Ballad of the Vicar of Bray

In good King Charles's golden days,
When Loyalty no harm meant;
A Furious High-Church man I was,
And so I gain'd Preferment.
Unto my Flock I daily Preach'd,
Kings are by God appointed,
And Damn'd are those who dare resist,
Or touch the Lord's Anointed.

And this is Law, I will maintain
Unto my Dying Day, Sir.
That whatsoever King may reign,
I will be the Vicar of Bray, Sir!

When Royal James possest the crown,
And popery grew in fashion;
The Penal Law I shouted down,
And read the Declaration:
The Church of Rome I found would fit
Full well my Constitution,
And I had been a Jesuit,
But for the Revolution.

And this is Law, &c.

When William our Deliverer came,
To heal the Nation's Grievance,
I turn'd the Cat in Pan again,
And swore to him Allegiance:
Old Principles I did revoke,
Set conscience at a distance,

Passive Obedience is a Joke,
A Jest is non-resistance.

And this is Law, &c.

When Royal Ann became our Queen,
Then Church of England's Glory,
Another face of things was seen,
And I became a Tory:
Occasional Conformists base
I Damn'd, and Moderation,
And thought the Church in danger was,
From such Prevarication.

And this is Law, &c.

When George in Pudding time came o'er,
And Moderate Men looked big, Sir,
My Principles I chang'd once more,
And so became a Whig, Sir.
And thus Preferment I procur'd,
From our Faith's great Defender,
And almost every day abjur'd
The Pope, and the Pretender.

And this is Law, &c.

The Illustrious House of Hannover,
And Protestant succession,
To these I lustily will swear,
Whilst they can keep possession:
For in my Faith, and Loyalty,
I never once will faulter,
But George, my lawful king shall be,
Except the Times shou'd alter.
And this is Law, &c.

The British Musical Miscellany, vol. I, 1734, text as
found in R. S. Crane, *A Collection of English Poems
1660–1800*, New York, Harper & Row

THE EARL OF SANDWICH

John Montagu, the fourth Earl of Sandwich, was an eighteenth-century peer who is best remembered for inadvertently inventing the sandwich. The story goes that on one occasion the Earl was so engrossed in a 24-hour gambling session (or it may have been a long working day at the Admiralty) that he sent a waiter to obtain slices of toasted bread and salted beef. To save time, he put the salted beef between two slices of bread and proceeded to eat the first sandwich.

Many scandals overshadowed his political ambitions. For example, he betrayed his one-time friend John Wilkes by reading out Wilkes's pornographic poetry in the House of Lords in order to discredit him.

Montagu was known as 'The Insatiable Earl' for his many excesses. He was a member of the Hell Fire Club, an exclusive collection of 24 aristocrats whose motto was 'Fay ce que voudras' (Do what you will). These rich young men formed themselves into the 'Monks of Medmenham' and conducted mock services in Medmenham in Buckinghamshire. On one occasion, the Earl was trying to summon up the devil and received the fright of his life when one of the members secretly released a baboon into their midst. The Earl thought he had succeeded in his invocation and fled in terror!

The Earl also kept his mistress, Martha Ray, at his estate in Hinchingbrooke House, for over 16 years and had five children with her, despite being married. In 1779, Martha was murdered at Covent Garden by a jealous admirer, Captain Hackman.

The Earl of Sandwich died in 1792 at the age of 74.

SAINTS AND SYMBOLS

Since early times, saints have had symbols associated with them in art to represent their lives and commemorate the manner of their martyrdom. Here are some saints and their symbols:

St Agnes

She was a devoted follower of Jesus who steadfastly refused all offers of marriage, claiming she was the 'bride of Christ'. She is now considered the patroness of chastity. Died AD 654.

St Athanasius

Athanasius was Bishop of Alexandria and a brilliant student of the Holy Scriptures. He was an authority on the ecclesiastical and canon laws of the Church and exerted a powerful influence on the Church. Died AD 373.

St Aidan

An Irish monk who was sent from the monastery on Iona to evangelize northern England; he received the devoted help of Kings Oswald and Oswin. Died AD 651.

St Augustine

Known as the 'Apostle of the English', Augustine and 40 monks brought the gospel to England. He was received by the pagan king, Ethelbert, who was soon baptized along with many others. Later Augustine was made bishop. Died AD 604.

St Alban

He was a pagan who sheltered a persecuted priest, and was then converted. He helped the priest to escape, whereupon the pagans' fury turned on Alban. He was beheaded in the city that now bears his name. Martyred about AD 303.

St Ambrose

This famous Bishop of Milan, one of the four Doctors of the Western Church, was a great lover of music. He added to the richness of sacred services of the Church via music, and introduced the antiphonal chants bearing his name today. Died AD 397.

St Antony of Padua

A faithful and eloquent preacher against doctrinal errors and wickedness, he is usually referred to as the 'hammer of heretics'. A follower of St Francis, he preached in France, Italy and Sicily until his death in Padua. Died AD 1231.

St Cyril of Alexandria

A native of Alexandria and patriarch of the city. Devoted much of his life to the defence of the truth of Christ's divinity. Died AD 444.

St Chrysostom

John, Bishop of Constantinople, became the most eloquent preacher of the early Church, and so was called Chrysostom, meaning 'Golden-mouthed'. Legend says that when he was a baby a swarm of bees settled on his mouth. Died AD 407.

St David

The patron saint of Wales, in which country he was born. He founded many monasteries, the most famous of which was in what is now St Davids. His monks followed a very austere rule. Died about AD 588.

St Columba (St Colum)

This saint founded many churches and monasteries in Ireland and Scotland, the most famous of which was on the island of Iona. One of the most consecrated and indefatigable of Christian missionaries. Died AD 597.

Dunstan

The English-born Dunstan became Abbot of Glastonbury. Legend says that the devil went to Dunstan's cell to tempt him, whereupon Dunstan caught the devil by the nose with red hot pincers and caused him to flee. Died AD 988.

St Gabriel

This archangel was the angel sent to Mary to announce that she was to be the mother of Jesus. He is sometimes called the 'Angel of the Annunciation' (Luke 1).

St George

St George is the patron saint of England and venerated as the model of knighthood and protector of women. He is also the patron of soldiers as for a long time he was a military man engaged in warfare with the pagans. Martyred AD 303.

St Katherine (Catherine) of Alexandria

She early converted to Christianity, and vanquished her pagan adversaries in a debate. This so enraged the Emperor that he ordered her to be put to death on a machine of spiked wheels. She was saved by a miracle, but was later beheaded. Martyred AD 310.

St Ignatius

Ignatius was Bishop of Antioch in Syria. When asked by the Emperor for a sacrifice to heathen gods, Ignatius refused. He was condemned and thrown to the wild beasts. Martyred 107 AD.

St Katherine (Catherine) of Siena

From childhood, Katherine was very religious, living at home in extreme self-mortification, and spending much time in prayer and meditation. Later she felt called to leave home and devoted herself to the care of the sick, and other good works. Died AD 1380.

St Michael

One of the archangels, St Michael is regarded traditionally as guardian of the Church and its members against the evil one. It is he who is supposed to weigh the souls of men at the Last Day.

St Lydia

A seller of purple dyes, Lydia was converted through the preaching of St Paul and was baptized, along with her whole household. She was the first recorded Christian convert in Europe (Acts 16. 14). Died in the first century.

St Nicholas

Bishop of Myra. Tradition says that St Nicholas went secretly to the house of a destitute nobleman three nights in succession and threw a purse of gold in the window. Patron saint of children. Died about AD 326.

St Martin

One day Martin saw a shivering beggar and shared his own cloak with this stranger. Later he entered the Church, and while Bishop of Tours he converted his whole area to Christianity. Died AD 401.

St Oswald

First of the English Royal Saints. As King of Northumbria, he diligently sought the complete evangelization of his country, and died fighting against a champion of paganism. Died AD 642.

St Patrick

A captive British boy in Ireland, Patrick escaped and was educated in Continental monasteries. Later he returned to Ireland to preach and teach the gospel and to build churches. Patron saint of Ireland. Died about AD 465.

St Timothy

Companion of Paul on his missionary journeys and referred to by Paul as 'the beloved son in faith'. Reputedly beaten and stoned to death for denouncing the worship of Diana. Died in the first century.

St Raphael

The archangel who is the guardian angel of all humanity. He is called the 'Healer of God' and is identified with the angel of the pool at Bethesda.

St Titus

A convert of St Paul, and mentioned in the Pauline epistles as his brother and co-partner in his labours. Reputedly the first Bishop of Crete. Died in the first century.

St Simeon

As a boy, Simeon joined the community of St John Stylites. For 69 years he lived on the top of pillars within the monastery, in the exercise of religious contemplation. Died about AD 597.

St Valentine

A priest who was active in assisting the martyrs in times of persecution. He was famous for the love and charity that he manifested. Martyred AD 269.

St Stephen

The Deacon and first Christian martyr, called by Luke 'a man full of faith and of the Holy Ghost.' Stoned to death in the first century.

Symbols of the Church, ed. Carroll E. Whittemore, with drawings by William Duncan, Nashville, USA, Abingdon Press, 1957.

PROTECTOR SAINTS

Catholics believe that praying to a particular saint who covers a cause, vocation or medical condition is beneficial. This is a selective list of saints showing the areas they cover. It cannot be a comprehensive list because in many cases more than one saint covers a particular area:

Occupation/Ailment	Saint
Accountants	Matthew
Actors	Genesius
Ague	Petronella
Astronauts	Joseph of Cupertino
Architects	Barbara
Artists	Luke
Authors	Sebastian
Bad dreams	Christopher

Bakers	Elizabeth of Hungary
Bankers	Matthew
Barren women	Antony of Padua
Bachelors	Christopher
Bee keepers	Ambrose
Beggars	Martin of Tours
Blacksmiths	Dunstan
Blind	Lucy
Blood banks	Janarius
Boils	Cosmus
Boy scouts	George
Brides	Nicholas of Myra
Bridegrooms	Nicholas of Myra
Breast cancer	Agatha
Brewers	Armand
Bricklayers	Stephen
Broadcasters	Archangel Gabriel
Butchers	Anthony of Egypt
Cab drivers	Fiacre
Carpenters	Joseph
Children	Agnes
Church	Joseph
Clerics	Gabriel
Cobblers	Bartholomew
Colic	Erasmus
Comedians	Vitus
Computer programmers	Isidore of Seville
Converts	Alban

Cooks	Lawrence
Cowboys	Bernard of Venice
Cripples	Giles
Dancers	Vitus
Death of children	Clotilde
Defilement	Susan
Dentists	Apollonia
Desperate situations	Jude
Dieticians	Martha
Doctors	Pantaleon
Dog bites	Vitus
Doubts	Catherine
Ecologists	Francis of Assisi
Epilepsy	Valentine
Fire fighters	Florian
Fishermen	Andrew
Funeral directors	Joseph of Arimathea
Gardeners	Fiacre
Girl Guides	Joan of Arc
Goldsmiths	Anastasius
Gout	Wolfgang
Grocers	Michael
Headaches	Theresa of Avila
Healers	Brigid of Ireland
Heart patients	John of God
Hopeless cases	Jude
Hospital administrators	Basil the Great
Hunters	Eustachius

Idiocy	Gildas
Infamy	Susan
Invalids	Roch
Jewellers	Eligius
Lawyers	Thomas More
Learning	Ambrose
Leprosy	Lazarus
Librarians	Jerome
Lost items	Antony of Padua
Lovers	Valentine
Married women	Monica
Mentally ill	Dympna
Messengers	Gabriel
Motorists	Anthony the Great
Musicians	Cecelia
Newlyweds	Dorothy
Nurses	Agatha
Orators	John Chrysostom
Palsy	Cornelius
Pawnbrokers	Nicholas
Philosophers	Justin
Physicians	Luke
Plague	Roch
Plasterers	Bartholomew
Poets	David
Police officers	Michael
Printers	John of God
Prisoners	Dismas

Quenching fire	Florian
Quinsy	Blaise
Radiologists	Michael
Rheumatism	James the Greater
Sailors	Brendan
Scabs	Rooke
Scientists	Albert the Great
Sculptors	Claude
Servants	Martha
Skaters	Lidwina
Skiers	Bernard
Skin diseases	Marculf
Sleepwalking	Dymphna
Smallpox	Martin of Tours
Soldiers	Martin of Tours
Sore eyes	Augustine of Hippo
Spinsters	Andrew
Storms	Barbara
Students	Thomas Aquinas
Sudden death	Martin of Tours
Sudden death	Barbara
Tailors	Homobonus
Television	Clare of Assisi
Theologians	Augustine
Throat ailments	Blaise
Toothache	Appolonia
Travellers	Christopher
Troubled families	Eustace

Unhappy husbands	Gomer
Unhappy wives	Uncumber
Venereal disease sufferers	Fiacre
Vermin	Huldrick
Victims of betrayal	Oswin
Victims of unfaithfulness	Catherine of Genoa
Widows	Frances of Rome
Widowers	Edgar
Wool combers	Blaise
Women in labour	Anne
Wealth	Anne

CHANG SHEN

Chinese evangelist Chang Shen (Blind Chang) lived in the Manchuria region of China in the late nineteenth century. Before his conversion to Christianity, Chang was a notorious thief, gambler and womanizer. Local villagers called him Wu So Pu Wei Te (Not an ounce of good), and when he was struck blind, neighbours reckoned it was a judgement from God.

When Chang heard of a missionary hospital hundreds of miles away where people were having their sight restored, he undertook an arduous journey lasting many days to see if they could help him. Unfortunately, all the hospital beds were taken, but the hospital chaplain gave Chang his own bed. There, Chang's physical and spiritual sight was restored as he received medical treatment and a Christian baptism.

Chang spread the gospel to his whole village upon his return, winning hundreds of converts. He committed most of the New Testament to memory, a necessary feat as his sight once again deteriorated.

During the early months of 1900, most of China rose up

against foreign 'devils' in a series of Boxer rebellions. When the Boxers reached Chang's village, they threatened to kill 50 people unless he was handed over to them. Chang was ready to embrace martyrdom and refused all attempts by his captors to worship Buddha.

No one knows when Chang died, but it is reported that as the Boxer leaders led him through the city walls to his death, he sang a hymn that he had learned at the mission hospital many years before that included these lines:

Jesus loves me, He who died Heaven's gate to open wide;
He will wash away my sin, Let His little child come in.
Jesus loves me, He will stay, Close beside me all the way;
If I love Him when I die, He will take me home on high.

ST ANGELA OF FOLIGNO

This saint is a great example of the power of repentance. Angela was born around 1284 and lived in the village of Foligno, about 10 miles from Assisi in Italy. She was a wealthy pagan who married young and had several children. She also lived a scandalous life and committed adultery with several lovers, producing yet more children.

However, in her thirties, her husband died and she experienced a moral crisis. She felt her sins were so great that she could not confess them such was her shame. So she prayed to St Francis of Assisi, who had died about 50 years before. He is said to have appeared to Angela in a dream, promising to help her.

Shortly after this, she met a Franciscan friar and she felt able to make a full confession to him. She underwent a conversion, did penance for her sins, and committed her life to the

Franciscan order. She made a pilgrimage to Rome, sold all her worldly goods, and became a Franciscan lay person.

Her new life led to many visionary experiences that are recorded in her writings – *Memoriale* and *Instructiones* – which she wrote for her sons and others who could learn from her experience. It is thought that she was endowed with the stigmata.

Today, Angela is invoked for many causes, including widows, the death of children, people ridiculed for their piety, and those suffering from sexual temptation. Curiously, she is also known as the 'Mistress of Theologians'.

> He [Christ] told me, 'Those of my little children who with-draw from my kingdom by their sinning and make them-selves sons of the devil, when they return to the Father, because he rejoices over their return, he demonstrates to them how especially joyful he is. Such indeed is his joy that he grants them a special grace that he does not grant to others who were virgins and had never gone away from him.

Extract from Memoriale

CHRISTIAN PIONEERS
IN SCIENCE

The twentieth century saw the worlds of faith and science move further and further apart. However, many pioneers of science were also faithful men who saw in scientific develop-ments many opportunities to testify to the glory of God. The hall of fame includes:

Name	Known for
Sir Francis Bacon (1561–1626)	Father of inductive reasoning

Johann Kepler (1571–1630)	Founder of physical astronomy
Robert Boyle (1627–1691)	Father of modern chemistry
Blaise Pascal (1623–1662)	Mathematician
John Ray (1627–1705)	Father of English natural history
Nicolaus Steno (1631–1686)	Founder of stratigraphy
William Petty (1623–1687)	Founder of statistics
Isaac Newton (1642–1727)	Discovered the law of gravity and inventor of the cat flap
Benjamin Franklin (1706–1790)	Invented the lightning rod
Carolus Linnaeus (1707–1778)	Founder of biological taxonomy
Johann Carl Friedrich Gauss	Discoverer of the law of quadratic reciprocity
Michael Faraday (1791–1867)	Inventor of the electrical generator
Charles Babbage (1792–1871)	Founder of computer science
John Dalton (1766–1844)	Invented atomic theory
Matthew Maury (1806–1873)	Father of oceanography
James Simpson (1811–1879)	Discovered chloroform
James Joule (1818–1889)	Father of thermo-dynamics
Gregory Mendel (1822–1884)	Father of genetics
Louis Pasteur (1822–1895	Father of bacteriology
Joseph Lister (1827–1912)	Founder of antiseptic surgery

Georg Cantor (1845–1918)	Discoverer of the theory of infinite sets
Thomas Edison (1847–1931)	Inventor of over 1,000 devices, including the phonograph and the light bulb
William Mitchell Ramsay (1851–1939)	Archaeologist
Georges Lemaître (1894–1966)	Formulated the Big Bang theory

HOLOCAUST HEROES

The story of Oscar Schindler has become well known through the Steven Spielberg film, *Schindler's List* (itself based on the 1982 book *Schindler's Ark* by Thomas Keneally). Schindler outwitted the Gestapo and saved more than 1,200 Jews from the Nazi death camps. It is heartening to know that Schindler's heroism was echoed by many others who defied Nazi attempts to exterminate the Jews. These Holocaust heroes include:

- Raoul Wallenberg, a Swedish diplomat based in Budapest in 1944–5. In defiance of Nazi rules, he issued 30,000 Jews with passes that enabled them to escape the Gestapo.

- Per Anger, another Swedish diplomat based in Budapest. He worked with Wallenberg to assist thousands of Jews to flee Hungary.

- Frederich Born, a Swiss national who saved over 12,000 Jews in Budapest by issuing them with Red Cross documents.

- Aristides de Sousa Mendes, a French diplomat based in

Bordeaux. Issued 30,000 passes to Jews, allowing them to escape to Portugal.

- Georg Ferdinand Duckwitz, a German diplomat based in Copenhagen. Risked his life by warning the Danish government of plans to deport Danish Jews. He is credited with saving over 7,000 Jews.

- Chiune Sugihara, a Japanese diplomat based in Lithuania. Issued hundreds of Jews with Japanese visas and saved over 1,000 people through his actions.

- Varian Fry, an American journalist. He established the American Relief Centre in Nazi France and rescued hundreds of refugees.

- Nicholas Winton, also known as the 'British Schindler'. He rescued 669 Czechs with help from the British Embassy in Prague. He was knighted in 2002.

SAINTLY OIL

It is said that some saints' relics have an oily substance flowing from them. The origin of this 'oil' is uncertain; it could be from lamps around the shrines of relics or from the relics themselves. The oil from the relics of St Martin of Tours and St Nicholas of Myra is said to have miraculous healing properties and was much sought after in the Middle Ages.

The saintly oil of St Walburga in Eichstadt in Bavaria, which is thought to be mostly water, has been used as a remedy against many diseases.

The oil of St Menas of Baumma in Libya made it a famous place of pilgrimage in the sixth century.

The tomb of St John the Evangelist was supposed to issue an oily substance in the seventh century. Similarly, the tomb of the Apostle Andrew was said to issue fragrant oil.

Other saints who are associated with this phenomenon include:

- St John the Almsgiver, Patriarch of Alexandria, d. 620 or 616.
- St John of Beverley, Bishop of York, d. 721.
- St Luke the Younger, a Greek hermit, d. 945–6.
- St Paul, Bishop of Verdun, d. 648.
- St Perpetuus, Bishop of Tongres-Utrecht, d. 630.
- St Reverianus, Bishop of Autun, and Companions, martyred about 273.
- St Sabinus, Bishop of Canosa, d. about 566.
- St Sigolena, Abbess of Troclar, d. about 700.
- St William, Archbishop of York, d. 1154.

ST MAMMERTUS AND ROGATION DAYS

St Mammertus was Archbishop of Vienne in Dauphine, France, in the fifth century. A learned scholar, he is chiefly remembered for reviving the series of fasts and prayers called 'Rogations' during the three days before the feast of the Ascension of Our Lord. Rogation comes from the Latin *rogatio* or *rogare*, meaning to beseech.

The idea of reviving Rogations came about in this way. The city of Vienne had been ravaged by wars, fires and earthquakes, and some considered these to be a divine judgement arising from the lax morals of the people. In the midst of these terrors, Mammertus prayed and received assurance of divine mercy. A terrible fire that was raging through Vienne suddenly ceased and the local people attributed this to a miracle resulting from Mammertus' prayers.

Mammertus decided that the practice of Rogations should be recommenced as a thanksgiving to God. In 475, the Church of Auvergne was used for this purpose, and very soon churches throughout the country had Rogation services. Pope Leo III recognized the importance of Rogation services shortly after, and today Rogation Sunday is still part of the church calendar. In some churches, the ancient date for Rogation Day (25 April) is still kept and referred to as Major Rogation Day, with the three days before Ascension known as Minor Rogation Days.

In the Middle Ages, it was common to perform the ceremony of 'beating the bounds' during Rogation Week. This was a formal procession of boys around the parish boundary, led by the parish priest. At the boundary points and other notable landmarks, scriptures were read, prayers were offered, and the boys were knocked against the boundary stones to make sure they remembered the parish limits! Elements of this ancient ceremony are still performed in many parishes today.

KING MANASSEH

King Manasseh was the thirteenth King of Judah and reigned in Israel for 55 years from 722 BC. His story is found in 2 Kings 21. 1–17 and 2 Chronicles 33. 1–20. Although Manasseh's father, Hezekiah, was a godly man, Manasseh is the most notorious of the Kings of Judah because of his evil acts, including:

- Sacrificing his children to heathen deities.
- Placing an idol in the temple.
- Getting rid of the Ark of the Covenant.
- Rebuilding pagan shrines.
- Murdering so many people that the streets of Jerusalem ran with blood.
- Leading his people astray 'so that they did more evil than the nations the LORD had destroyed before the Israelites' (2 Chronicles 33. 9).

This wicked man was eventually imprisoned by the Assyrians who humiliated him by taking him into exile. In his distress, Manasseh confessed his sins and turned to the Lord. Amazingly, he was restored to his throne where he set about undoing all his evil ways. He destroyed the pagan shrines, removed his idols from the temple, and restored temple worship. However, Judah still had to face the consequences of Manasseh's reign and the subsequent fall of the kingdom is blamed on Manasseh.

The story of Manasseh affords a wonderful lesson about God's mercy. Even a thoroughly wicked man like Manasseh was heard by God because of his humility and earnest repentance. Manasseh's life shows that no one is wholly excluded from God's provision and, whatever our past deeds, God is looking to forgive us and restore us as we acknowledge his ways:

> Manasseh was twelve years old when he became king, and he reigned in Jerusalem for fifty-five years. He did evil in the eyes of the LORD, following the detestable practices of the nations the LORD had driven out before the Israelites. He rebuilt the high places his father Hezekiah had demolished; he also erected altars to the Baals and made Asherah poles. He bowed down to all the starry hosts and worshipped them. He built altars in the temple of the LORD, of which the LORD had said, 'My Name will remain in Jerusalem for ever.' In both courts of the temple of the LORD, he built altars to all the starry hosts. He sacrificed his sons in the fire in the Valley of Ben Hinnom, practised sorcery, divination and witchcraft, and consulted mediums and spiritists. He did much evil in the eyes of the LORD, provoking him to anger (2 Chronicles 33. 1–6).

> In his distress he sought the favour of the LORD his God and humbled himself greatly before the God of his fathers. And when he prayed to him, the LORD was moved by his entreaty and listened to his plea; so he brought him back to Jerusalem and to his kingdom. Then Manasseh knew that the LORD is God (2 Chronicles 33. 12–13).

FAMOUS RELICS

According to the legend, when the Emperor Charlemagne had finished building the church of Our Lady in Aix-la-Chapelle, France, he set himself the task of collecting famous relics from Rome, Constantinople, Jerusalem and other centres of Christendom.

Among the relics he managed to obtain were:

- The tunic of the Blessed Virgin.
- The swaddling-clothes of the infant Jesus.
- The loincloth worn by Jesus on the cross.
- The cloth in which the head of St John the Baptist was enveloped after his decapitation.
- A small piece of the cord with which Christ was bound during the flagellation.
- The girdle of the Virgin.
- A bit of the sponge that was offered to Christ on the cross.
- A lock of hair from the head of St Bartholomew.
- Two of St Thomas the Apostle's teeth.
- One of the arms of the old Simeon.
- A fragment of the cross.
- A tooth of St Catherine.
- The point of a nail with which Christ was attached to the cross.
- A bit of the rod that served in the mocking of Christ.
- A lock of hair from the head of St John the Baptist.

These relics were exhibited every seven years during the period 10 to 24 July and drew enormous crowds.

The tunic of the Virgin was said to be yellowish in colour, 5½ feet in length, and 3¼ feet in circumference, with a small amount of decoration. The swaddling-clothes of the infant Jesus were folded three times in double folds and had brownish yellow ribbons. The blood-stained linen of St John the Baptist was of fine texture, folded and bound with red ribbons. The linen cloth that was bound round Christ's loins upon the cross was of a heavy texture, folded, and was very blood-stained. It was folded in a triangular shape, 4 feet 2½ inches in length, and 4 feet 10 inches in width.

ST VALENTINE

Little is known about this celebrated saint, but it is thought he was a fourth-century Roman who was martyred during the reign of Claudius II. His feast day, on 14 February, supersedes the ancient Roman festival of Lupercalia when young men and women drew lots for one another.

Valentine is the saint of lovers, and in former times it was the custom for men to send presents to their sweethearts. In some places, it was the tradition that the gentleman's valentine was the first lady he saw on Valentine's Day – and vice versa for ladies.

In England in the eighteenth century, the eve of St Valentine's Day was celebrated thus: an equal number of maids and bachelors came together, with each writing their true love's name, and a feigned name, upon separate tickets. These were rolled up and lots were drawn, so that each girl was randomly matched to each lad, and each lad matched to each girl. By this means, everyone had two partners, but the lad had to select the valentine. The couples then spent the next few days feasting and dancing.

Many songs, poems and ballads were sung on St Valentine's Day, including this invocation to the saint:

Hast, friendly Saint! to my relief,
My heart is stol'n, help! stop the thief!
My rifled breast I search'd with care,
And found Eliza lurking there.
Away she started from my view,
Yet may be caught, if thou pursue;
Nor need I to describe her strive –

The fairest, dearest maid alive!
Seize her – yet treat the nymph divine
With gentle usage, Valentine!
Then, tell her, she, for what was done,
Must bring my heart, and give her own.

Samuel Pepys noted Valentine's Day 1667 thus: 'This morning came up to my wife's bedside (I being up dressing myself) little Will Mercer to be her valentine, and brought her name written upon blue paper in gold letters, done by himself, very pretty; and we were both well pleased with it. But I am also this year my wife's valentine, and it will cost me £5: but that I must have laid out if we had not been valentines.'

ST PAUL THE SIMPLE

This saint is thus called because he did not have of the gifts of intellect or high learning. He lived in the second century as a hermit in Egypt, but his calling came at great cost.

It is said that he journeyed for eight days into the desert to become a disciple of St Antony. But Antony would not accept him, and told him to return home. However, Paul fasted, prayed and waited at Antony's door until he was admitted. In order to test Paul's commitment, Antony put many trials in his way, including:

- Asking him to undo his diligent work of making mats and begin all over again.
- Spilling honey in the desert sand and asking Paul to gather it up without any grain of sand in it.
- Ordering him to sew and unsew garments.
- Go seven days without eating.

Even after he proved himself through these trials, Paul was only allowed a cell some 3 miles distant from Antony. It is said that Paul cured many sick and demon-possessed people in the desert. He died around 330.

SOLSTICE SAINTS

Before the advent of artificial light dulled our sense of the importance of seasons, the two solstices marked key turning points in the year. The winter solstice occurs in dark days in the Northern Hemisphere, when all of nature seems static. The summer solstice promises warmth and light, but with the knowledge that the sun has already reached its greatest strength.

In ancient times, the festivals of saints around the time of the winter and summer solstice were particularly important as they gave the opportunity to replace pagan traditions with Christian customs.

There are three main solstice saints, these being:

- St Lucy (meaning light), whose feast day on 13 December marked the winter solstice in the old calendar. The customary rhyme, 'Lucy-light, shortest day and longest night', connects the saint to the winter solstice. Lucy is honoured as a virgin martyr who refused marriage to a pagan and was killed in 304. She is the patron saint of all who have eye diseases, because she was supposed to have been blinded by her tormentors. Swedish people call Lucy's Day 'Little Yule' because it falls near the season of Advent. On Lucy's Day, most Swedish rural households used to choose the youngest girl to be the Lucia Queen. She had to rise early and wake everyone up with her special song and then hand out gifts of food. In many parts of Europe, St Lucy was sometimes the companion of St Nicholas as the bringer of gifts.

- Thomas the Apostle (Doubting Thomas) has his feast day

on 21 December. Because of his doubting nature, in many parts of Europe Thomas was represented as a mysterious figure of light and dark. He is invoked for protection against witches, but also associated with calling the dead to rise from their graves. St Thomas's Day was greatly celebrated in schools because it was the custom to lock the doors to shut the schoolteachers out! Instead of lessons, the children took to play and sang, as for example in rural Scotland: 'This is the shortest day, an' we maun hae the play; an' if ye wunna gies the play, we'll steek ye oot a the day!'

- John the Baptist is the saint of the summer solstice, his feast day being Midsummer Day, 24 June. Bonfires were lit in his honour across the hilltops in many European countries, and there used to be grand parades to commemorate his life. It was thought that a barren woman who walked naked in her garden at midnight to gather St John's Wort would conceive within a year. John the Baptist is the patron saint of bird dealers, epileptics, farriers, lambs and motorways.

ST ELIZABETH ANN SETON

 Elizabeth Ann Seton is known as the first American-born saint. She was beatified in 1963 and canonized in 1975 for her work in founding the Sisters of Charity Mission in America – the first religious community for women in that nation.

She was born into a committed Episcopalian family in 1774 in New York, but lost her mother and a younger sister while still a child – a fate she bore with customary courage and steadfast hope.

She married a wealthy businessman, William Magee Seton, at 19 and had five children. However, he died of tuberculosis while visiting Italy and she was reduced to living the life of a penniless widow with five children to support. Elizabeth adopted the Catholic faith in March 1805, after visiting Italy with her husband.

Although poor, in partnership with her sister-in-law, Rebecca, Elizabeth founded the Society for the Relief of Poor Widows with Small Children. With help from her friends, she also opened a boarding school for boys (St Joseph's Academy and Free School) and then a similar school for girls. These institutions were run along the lines of a religious order and eventually became a community of nuns.

The order of nuns grew and quickly expanded in other areas to serve as hospitals, orphanages and schools. Elizabeth died in 1821 and is buried in Emmitsburg, Maryland. She is remembered on 4 January in the calendar of saints.

What stands out about Elizabeth Ann Seton is her ordinariness – she was not a mystic or stigmatic. She had no great spiritual gifts, but accomplished much because she abandoned herself to God, as is made clear by one of her most famous quotes: 'The first end I propose in our daily work is to do the will of God; secondly, to do it in the manner he wills it; and thirdly, to do it because it is his will.'

MEXICAN MARTYRS

After years of civil war and revolutionary struggle, the year 1917 witnessed a new Mexican constitution initiated by President Venustiano Carranza. Although in theory this gave freedom of expression to all faiths, the years that followed were a period of intense religious persecution because of the chaotic state of the country, characterized by tribal violence, rampant inflation, food shortages and poor communications.

The nationalistic government expelled foreign priests, a move that led to the formation of a guerrilla organization called the 'Cristero Movement'. It was during these years of struggle that many priests were murdered, including the following 25 martyrs:

Name	Date
Fr Cristóbal Magallanes Jara	Shot on 25 May 1927
Fr Agustín Caloca Cortés	Shot on 25 May 1927
Fr José Maria Robles Hurtado	Hanged on 26 June 1927
Fr David Galván Bermúdez	Shot on 30 January 1915
Fr Justino Orona Madrigal	Shot on 1 July 1928
Fr Atilano Cruz Alvarado	Shot on 1 July 1928
Fr Román Adame Rosales	Shot on 21 April 1927
Fr Julio Álvarez Mendoza	Shot on 30 March 1927
Fr Pedro Esqueda Ramírez	Shot on 22 November 1927
Fr Rodrigo Aguilar Alemán	Hanged on 28 October 1927
Fr Tranquilino Ubiarco Robles	Hanged on 5 October 1928
Fr Jenaro Sánchez Delgadillo	Hanged on 17 January 1927
Fr José Isabel Flores Varela	Beheaded on 21 June 1927
Fr Sabás Reyes Salazar	Shot on 13 April 1927
Fr Toribio Romo González	Shot on 25 February 1928
Fr Luis Batiz	Shot on 15 August 1926
Manuel Morales	Shot on 15 August 1926
Salvador Lara Puente	Shot on 15 August 1926
David Roldán Lara	Shot on 15 August 1926
Fr Mateo Correa Magallanes	Shot on 6 February 1927
Fr Pedro de Jesús Maldonado	Shot on 11 February 1937

Fr Jesús Méndez Montoya	Shot on 5 February 1928
Fr David Uribe Velasco	Shot on 12 April 1927
Fr Margarito Flores García	Shot on 12 November 1927
Fr Miguel de la Mora	Shot on 7 August 1927

On 22 November 1992 these martyrs were beatified and on 21 May 2000 they were canonized by Pope John Paul II. Today, over 95 per cent of the population in Mexico classifies itself as Christian.

> Be faithful, even to the point of death, and I will give you the crown of life.
>
> *Revelation 2. 10*

ST MONICA –
LAPSED CATHOLICS

 St Monica (331–88) is known as the patron saint of lapsed Catholics and unfaithful husbands. More famously, she is the mother of Augustine the Great, Bishop of Hippo. However, her brilliant son was very self-willed and for 12 years left the Catholic faith and joined a heretical sect called the Manichees, where he lived an immoral life and refused to be baptized. During this time, she also had to contend with her husband, Patricius, who was a bad-tempered pagan given to having affairs with other women.

She was so angry with Augustine that she kicked him out of the house and pleaded every day with God for his return to the Catholic faith. She did not nag Patricius, but let him see – by the example of her life – how true happiness can be experienced. A year before his death, Patricius was converted.

When Augustine left for Rome to become a teacher of rhetoric, Monica continued faithfully in prayer for him and eventually joined him in Milan. There her prayers were answered, when Augustine abandoned the Manichees and accepted the Catholic faith in 386. Her words to Augustine upon his turning to the Catholic faith, a few days before she died, are recorded in *Augustine's Confessions*: 'Now my hopes in this world are accomplished. One thing there was for which I desired to linger for a while in this life, that I might see thee a Catholic Christian before I died. My God hath done this for me more abundantly, that I should now see thee withal despising earthly happiness.'

SHE WHO MOVES FORWARD

Kateri Tekakwitha is the first native American to become a saint. She was a born into the Turtle Clan of the Iroquois tribe in 1656 along the south bank of the Mohawk River near a village called Ossernenon. It is thought that her mother was a Christian and her name, Tekakwitha, means 'she who moves forward', or 'she who puts things in order'.

Before her fifth birthday, Kateri survived a smallpox epidemic that claimed the lives of her parents and baby brother. But the disease impaired her vision and scarred her face. Following the death of her parents, she was raised by tribal parents.

In 1667 the area was visited by Jesuit missionaries (known as the Blackrobes) and she came to a knowledge of the Christian faith through this contact. The Blackrobes established a mission nearby and, despite tribal opposition, she was baptized on 5 April 1676, taking the name Kateri (Indian for Catherine).

She suffered persecution from her tribe and eventually had to flee the encampment, with the help of other Christian Indians. She remained a steadfast Christian despite much opposition and died on 17 April 1680 at the age of 24.

The case for her canonization was started in 1884 under Pope Leo XIII and she was beatified by Pope John Paul II on 22 June 1980. She is recognized as the patron saint of ecologists, exiles, orphans and people ridiculed for their faith.

YOU DON'T HAVE TO BE A ROCKET SCIENTIST TO BE THE PATRON SAINT OF ASTRONAUTS

Joseph Desa, who became St Joseph of Cupertino, patron saint of astronauts, had nothing to commend him as a child. This Franciscan friar, born on 17 June 1603 near Brindisi, Italy, was also known as Joseph the Dunce.

As a child, he received ecstatic visions but did not know what to make of them. He was useless at school, absent minded, awkward, a poor speaker and nervous. He was not wanted as a child and his slowness made him more and more isolated at home.

Without any hope of a vocation, he tried to become a monk and was initially refused because of his lack of education. When he was accepted as a lay brother in 1620, the monks found they could not do anything with him because of his ecstatic visions, which rendered him insensible. When he received a vision, it was as if Joseph turned to stone and the monks had to prick him with needles to enable him to return to the real world.

He could barely read or write, but his devotion to Christ led to a series of extraordinary visions and miraculous healings. It is said that he would often levitate (hence the connection to astronauts) while experiencing these visions and had a deep understanding of the mysteries of faith. He seemed to have a discerning heart and was able to communicate with animals in much the same way as Francis of Assisi. Moreover, despite his disadvantages he was a cheerful soul, often caught up in the experience of God.

However, because of the controversy surrounding his ecstasies, he was not allowed to be in the choir or eat with the other monks and was placed in his own cell so that he didn't embarrass the other monks. He was even questioned by the Spanish Inquisition, but did not allow their threats to take away his joyous spirit.

He died on 18 September 1663 and was canonized in 1767 by Pope Clement XIII. His life exemplifies the sovereign choice of God, as found in 1 Corinthians:

> But God chose the foolish things of the world to shame the wise; God chose the weak things of the world to shame the strong. He chose the lowly things of this world and the despised things – and the things that are not – to nullify the things that are, so that no one may boast before him.
>
> *1 Corinthians 1. 27–9*

A MODERN RELIC CERTIFICATE

Although most relics belong to the Middle Ages, they are still widely used as objects of devotion in the Roman Catholic and Orthodox Churches. It is still possible to obtain a relic (from a 'relic bank' in Rome), although it is forbidden under church law to charge for a relic (apart from a charge for the required relic case). In most cases, the relic provided is a very small piece of bone or skin, accompanied by a certificate of authenticity signed by the Keeper of Relics. The example below is a relatively modern certificate for relics from St Valentine sent from Rome to Dublin.

Translation of letter accompanying the remains of St Valentine:

St Valentine

We, Charles, by the divine mercy, Bishop of Sabina of the Holy Roman Church, Cardinal Odescalchi arch priest of the sacred Liberian Basilica, Vicar General of our most Holy Father the Pope and Judge in ordinary of the Roman Curia and of its districts, etc., etc.

To all and everyone who shall inspect these our present letters, we certify and attest, that for the greater glory of the omnipotent God and the veneration of his saints, we have freely given to the Very Reverend Father Spratt, Master of Sacred Theology of the Order of Calced Carmelites of the convent of that Order at Dublin, in Ireland, the blessed body of St Valentine, martyr, which we ourselves by the command of the most Holy Father Pope Gregory XVI on the 27th day of December 1835, have taken out of the cemetery of St Hyppolytus in the Tiburtine Way, together with a small vessel tinged with his blood and have deposited them in a wooden case covered with painted paper, well closed, tied with a red silk ribbon and sealed with our seals and we have so delivered and consigned to him, and we have granted unto him power in the Lord, to the end that he may retain to himself, give to others, transmit beyond the city (Rome) and in any church, oratory or chapel, to expose and place the said blessed holy body for the public veneration of the faithful without, however, an Office and Mass, conformably to the decree of the Sacred Congregation of Rites, promulgated on the 11th day of August 1691.

In testimony whereof, these letters, testimonial subscribed with our hand, and sealed with our seal, we have directed to be expedited by the undersigned keeper of sacred relics.

Rome, from our Palace, the 29th day of the
month of January 1836.

RULE OF ST COLUMBA

The Church in Ireland stands as a shining light in the early Middle Ages. As a European monastic centre, it had no equals to match its missionary zeal, and faithful men such as St Columba and his followers went to Scotland to convert the heathen. Their influence stretched throughout northern Europe as many people left their pagan ways and embraced Christianity.

St Columba and his monks did not leave any written rules, preferring the guidance of Scripture to direct them. However, the following 'rule', attributed to St Columba, was practised much later and it shows the depth of the Irish faith:

- Be alone in a separate place near a chief city, if thy conscience is not prepared to be in common with the crowd.
- Be always naked in imitation of Christ and the Evangelists.
- Whatsoever little or much thou possess of anything, whether clothing, or food, or drink, let it be at the command of the senior and at his disposal, for it is not befitting a religious to have any distinction of property with his own free brother.
- Let a fast place, with one door, enclose thee.
- A few religious men to converse with thee of God and his Testament; to visit thee on days of solemnity; to strengthen thee in the Testaments of God, and the narratives of the Scriptures.
- A person too who would talk with thee in idle words, or of the world; or who murmurs at what he cannot remedy or prevent, but who would distress thee more should he be a tattler between friends and foes, thou shalt not admit him to thee, but at once give him thy benediction should he deserve it.
- Let thy servant be a discreet, religious, not tale-telling man, who is to attend continually on thee, with moderate labour of course, but always ready.
- Yield submission to every rule that is of devotion.
- A mind prepared for red martyrdom [that is death for the faith].

- A mind fortified and steadfast for white martyrdom [that is ascetic practices]. Forgiveness from the heart of every one.
- Constant prayers for those who trouble thee.
- Fervour in singing the office for the dead, as if every faithful dead was a particular friend of thine.
- Hymns for souls to be sung standing.
- Let thy vigils be constant from eve to eve, under the direction of another person.
- Three labours in the day, viz., prayers, work, and reading.
- The work to be divided into three parts, viz., thine own work, and the work of thy place, as regards its real wants; secondly, thy share of the brethen's [work]; lastly, to help the neighbours, viz., by instruction or writing, or sewing garments, or whatever labour they may be in want of, ut Dominus ait, 'Non apparebis ante Me vacuus [as the Lord says, 'You shall not appear before me empty'].
- Everything in its proper order; Nemo enim coronabitur nisi qui legitime certaverit. [For no one is crowned except he who has striven lawfully.]
- Follow alms-giving before all things.
- Take not of food till thou art hungry.
- Sleep not till thou feelest desire.
- Speak not except on business.
- Every increase which comes to thee in lawful meals, or in wearing apparel, give it for pity to the brethren that want it, or to the poor in like manner.
- The love of God with all thy heart and all thy strength.
- The love of thy neighbour as thyself.
- Abide in the Testament of God throughout all times.
- Thy measure of prayer shall be until thy tears come.
- Or thy measure of work of labour till thy tears come.
- Or thy measure of thy work of labour, or of thy genuflexions, until thy perspiration often comes, if thy tears are not free.

A. W. Haddan and W. Stubbs, Councils and Ecclesiastical Documents Relating to Great Britain and Ireland II, vol. i, *Oxford, Oxford University Press, 1873, pp. 119–21.*

THE FICTITIOUS SAINT

 It is thought that the legend of St Urho was created in 1956 by Richard Mattson, a retail store manager from Virginia in the USA as a rival to St Patrick. His joke story of the patron saint of Finland quickly gained credence and today St Urho's Day is celebrated in Finnish centres in Virginia, Minnesota and New York as well as cities in Finland.

Mattson's story was a simple retelling based on the legend of St Patrick, who is said to have expelled snakes from Ireland. In Mattson's version, St Urho was famous for driving out poisonous frogs from Finland! In some later versions, it is supposed to be grasshoppers rather than frogs.

It is thought that Mattson called the saint after Urho Kekkonen who became the President of Finland in March 1956. According to Mattson, Urho was a powerful man who gained his strength from fish soup (*kalla mojakka*)and sour whole milk (*feelia sour*).

There are varied rituals and ceremonies on St Urho's Day on 16 March that include Finnish national dishes, dressing up as grasshoppers, and wearing the saint's colours – purple and green. It is a day to party and celebrate all things Finnish. There is even an Ode to St Urho that is sometimes recited:

Ooksie, kooksie kollme vee
Santia Urho is the boy for me
He chase out the hopper as big as birds
Never before have I heard those words.

He really told those bugs of green.
Bravest Finn I ever seen.
Some celebrate for St Pat and his snake
But that Urho boy got what it takes.

He got tall and strong on *feelia sour*
And ate *kalla mojakka* every hour.
That's why that guy could chase those beetles
That crew as thick as jack pine needles.

So let's give a cheer
in our very best way
On the sixteenth of March
St Urho's Day!

(Incidentally, Finland's official national patron saint is Henry of Uppsala.)

THE CHIEF OF SINNERS

John Bunyan, the famous author of *The Pilgrim's Progress* and a spiritual giant, was born in Bedford in 1628. When he reached 16, he joined Cromwell's New Model Army and then became a tinker. Upon leaving military service, he joined the Puritan Free Church in Bedford and became a 'field preacher'.

This was a dangerous occupation in the reign of King Charles II and, in 1666, Bunyan was imprisoned in Bedford for his evangelical activities. While in prison, he wrote his spiritual autobiography – *Grace Abounding to the Chief of Sinners* – describing the spiritual change that occurred in his life from being a profane unbeliever to a fervent preacher and author. This extract from that book finds Bunyan typically expressing his lack of trust in himself (he referred to himself as 'a poor and contemptible servant of Jesus Christ') and his enduring need for God's grace:

I find to this day seven abominations in my heart: (1)

Inclinings to unbelief. (2) Suddenly to forget the love and mercy that Christ manifesteth. (3) A leaning to the works of the law. (4) Wanderings and coldness in prayer. (5) To forget to watch for that I pray for. (6) Apt to murmur because I have no more, and yet ready to abuse what I have. (7) I can do none of those things which God commands me, but my corruptions will thrust in themselves, 'When I would do good, evil is present with me.'

These things I continually see and feel, and am afflicted and oppressed with; yet the wisdom of God doth order them for my good. (1) They make me abhor myself. (2) They keep me from trusting my heart. (3) They convince me of the insufficiency of all inherent righteousness. (4) They show me the necessity of flying to Jesus. (5) They press me to pray unto God. (6) They show me the need I have to watch and be sober. (7) And provoke me to look to God, through Christ, to help me, and carry me through this world.

SEVEN DEADLY SINS, HEAVENLY VIRTUES, AND CORPORAL WORKS OF MERCY

Deadly Sins	Heavenly virtues	Corporal works of mercy
Pride	Faith	Feed the hungry
Envy	Hope	Give drink to the thirsty
Gluttony	Charity	Give shelter to strangers
Lust	Fortitude	Clothe the naked
Anger	Justice	Visit the sick
Greed	Temperance	Minister to prisoners
Sloth	Prudence	Bury the dead

TEN TWENTIETH-CENTURY MARTYRS

On 9 July 1998, the Archbishop of Canterbury, in the presence of Queen Elizabeth II, unveiled statues of ten twentieth-century martyrs outside the west front of Westminster Abbey. The ten martyrs commemorated were:

- Father Maximilian Kolbe (Zdunska Wola), a victim of Nazism in 1941. He offered his own life to save a fellow prisoner, Franciszek Gajowniczek, condemned to death by the camp authorities after a successful escape by a fellow prisoner.

- Manche Masemola, murdered by her parents for converting to Christianity in Transvaal (South Africa) in 1928.

- Janani Luwum, a school teacher from Uganda, murdered in 1976 by the Idi Amin regime.

- Grand Duchess Elizabeth of Russia, a victim of the Russian Revolution of 1918.

- Dr Martin Luther King Jnr, American preacher assassinated in Memphis in 1968.

- Archbishop Oscar Romero of San Salvador, murdered in 1980.

- Dietrich Bonhoeffer, German pastor murdered by the Nazis in April 1945.

- Esther John (Qamar Zia), Indian missionary, murdered in 1960.

- Lucian Tapiedi, from Papua New Guinea, murdered by Japanese troops in 1942.

- Wang Zhiming, Chinese pastor, executed by the authorities in 1973.

BIBLICAL TERMS FOR SIN

What is sin? The Bible uses many different terms to cover the basic tendency to do wrong that is inherent in every person. The Bible provides a comprehensive explanation for the existence of sin and how we can be set free from it now and for ever more. Here are some biblical terms for this much misunderstood and sorry state:

- The Old Testament has at least 8 Hebrew words to describe sin – *ra* meaning 'bad', *rasha* meaning 'wickedness', *asham* meaning 'guilt', *chata* meaning 'sin', *avon* meaning 'iniquity', *shagag* meaning 'err', *taah* meaning 'wander away', and *pasha* meaning 'rebel'. Perhaps the last term best describes the overall 'drive' of sin – it is rebellion against that which is right and true.

- The New Testament has at least 12 Greek terms to describe sin, including *kakos* meaning 'bad', *poneros* meaning 'evil', *absebes* meaning 'godless', *enochos* meaning 'guilt', *adikia* meaning 'unrighteousness', *agnoein* meaning 'ignorant', *anomos* meaning 'lawlessness', *parabtes* meaning 'transgression', *planan* meaning 'to go astray', *paratoma* meaning 'to fall away', and *hupocrites*, meaning 'hypocrite'.

The Bible does not make a distinction between serious (mortal) and not so serious (venial) sins, although the Catholic Church teaches this as one of its doctrines. The remedy of salvation by faith in Jesus, based upon the Grace of God, saves sinners from the penalty, punishment and presence of sin.

These truths are admirably expressed in Charles Wesley's popular hymn, 'Ye Ransomed Sinners Hear':

> Ye ransomed sinners, hear,
> The prisoners of the Lord;
> And wait till Christ appear
> According to His Word.

Rejoice in hope; rejoice with me.
Rejoice in hope; rejoice with me.

We shall from all our sins be free.
In God we put our trust:
If we our sins confess,
Faithful He is, and just,
From all unrighteousness
To cleanse us all, both you and me;
To cleanse us all, both you and me;

We shall from all our sins be free.
Surely in us the hope
Of glory shall appear;
Sinners, your heads lift up
And see redemption near.
Again I say: rejoice with me.
Again I say: rejoice with me.

ST BARTHOLOMEW'S DAY
MASSACRE

On 24 August 1572 (St Bartholomew's Day), a great persecution began against French Protestants (Huguenots). The
Huguenots (meaning 'sworn companions') were followers
of John Calvin, who led a growing movement away from
papal authority throughout France. These believers were
encouraged in their endeavours by many French nobles and it
seemed, for a time, that a substantial Protestant Church along
the lines of Calvin's Geneva church could be established in
France.

However, the growth of the Huguenots caused alarm at the
Vatican and among the French court. Queen Catherine de'
Medici demanded the death of the Huguenot leader, Admiral
Coligny. This took place while the Queen's daughter,

Marguerite de Valois, was exchanging marriage vows with the Protestant Henry de Bourbon (King of Navarre – later King Henry IV). Indeed the wedding celebrations marked the start of a massacre that claimed the lives of thousands of Protestants, and Henry de Bourbon was the sole Huguenot survivor from the wedding party.

Anti-Huguenot violence spread from Paris throughout France leading to at least 30,000 deaths. This is part of an eye-witness account from the statesman and historian Jacques Auguste de Thou:

So it was determined to exterminate all the Protestants, and the plan was approved by the queen. They discussed for some time whether they should make an exception of the king of Navarre. All agreed that the king of Navarre should be spared by reason of the royal dignity and the new alliance. The Duke of Guise, who was put in full command of the enterprise, summoned by night several captains of the Catholic Swiss mercenaries from the five little cantons, and some commanders of French companies, and told them that it was the will of the king that, according to God's will, they should take vengeance on the band of rebels while they had the beasts in the toils.

After Coligny had said his prayers with Merlin the minister, he said, without any appearance of alarm, to those who were present: 'I see clearly that which they seek, and I am ready steadfastly to suffer that death which I have never feared and which for a long time past I have pictured to myself. I consider myself happy in feeling the approach of death and in being ready to die in God, by whose grace I hope for the life everlasting. For me it is enough that God is here, to whose goodness I commend my soul, which is so soon to issue from my body'.

Readings in European History, *ed. J. H. Robinson,*
Boston: Ginn, 1906, pp. 179–83.

THE FORMULAE OF
ST EUCHERIUS

St Eucherius was the Bishop of Lyon in the fifth century. A noted scholar, he is known today for his 'formulas of spiritual intelligence' – a series of 'biblical proofs' in the style of logical statements. Eucherius believed, 'The divine scriptures first shine like silver but glow like gold in their hidden parts. Rightly it is so managed, because the purity of eloquence is hidden altogether from the promiscuous eyes of the crowd, as if it were covered by a garment of modesty. And so, the divine is taken care of by the best stewardship; the scriptures themselves protect the heavenly mysteries by cloaking them, just as divinity itself works in its own mysterious way.'

He wrote a series of formulae and this is an extract from the one entitled 'Names and Significance of the Members of the Lord':

> The eyes of the Lord are understood by divine examination; Psalm 33: the eyes of the Lord are toward the righteous.
> The ears of the Lord are worthy when they hear; Psalm 33: his ears are toward their cries.
> The arms of the Lord are a help to his saints; Psalm 34: take up arms and a shield.
> The protection of the Lord is a shield; Psalm 5: O Lord, you have crowned us with the shield of your goodwill.
> The precepts of the Lord or of the Apostles are arrows; Psalm 17: he has sent his arrows and has scattered them.
> The word of the Lord is living, and it is as efficacious and penetrating as a two-edged sword. (Hebrews. 4. 12)
> The trumpet of God is the voice of the Lord made manifest; in the command and voice of the archangel and in the trumpet of God. (1 Thess. 4. 15)
> The rod of the Lord is a sign of his rule or of the correction of discipline; Psalm 45: the rod of equity, the rod of your reign.

The staff of the Lord is the sustaining consolation of God; Psalm 23: your rod and your staff, they comfort me.

Fire is the Holy Spirit; Acts 2: and fire appeared to them in forked tongues and sat above each of them, and they were filled with the Holy Spirit.

THE LITTLE FLOWER OF JESUS

Marie-Françoise-Thérèse Martin, who is revered as St Teresa of Lisieux (France), is the latest Doctor of the Church. Born in 1873, this 'little flower of Jesus' only lived to the age of 23, but achieved much in her short life.

She entered the Carmelite order in Lisieux when she was just 15. The closeness of her walk with Jesus is attested to by her much loved writings. A childlike faith, a constant seeking after spiritual growth, knowledge of the Scriptures and her humility are the hallmarks of her 'little way'.

As an adolescent, Teresa yearned to be a saint and sought God to attain ever more holinesss – 'I desire to be a saint, but I know my weakness and so I ask you, my God, that you yourself be my holiness' – is one of her most famous sayings. She experienced a powerful conversion on Christmas Day 1886, after attending midnight Mass.

Unlike many other saints, there are no miracles recorded during Teresa's life, no special signs or great conflicts with secular authorities. Yet her ordinary existence attracts many pilgrims to Lisieux who come to celebrate her extraordinary relationship with God. Almost all we know of Teresa is through her writings (over 250 letters, 54 poems, 8 plays, over 20 prayers, and her 'Final Conversations') which began to be published a year after her death. Today, there are more than 50 editions of her works, and in 1993 her *Complete Works* were presented to Pope John Paul II.

This is an extract from a poem called 'My Hope', first published in 1896:

> Though in a foreign land I dwell afar,
> I taste in dreams the endless joys of heaven.
> Fain would I fly beyond the farthest star,
> And see the wonders to the ransomed given!
> No more the sense of exile weighs on me,
> When once I dream of that immortal day.
> To my true fatherland, dear God! I see,
> For the first time I soon shall fly away.

THE LEPER OF MOLOKAI

On 11 May 1873 the steamer *Kilauea* deposited 33-year-old Father Joseph Damien de Veuster on the landing at Molokai in the Hawaiian Islands. The Islands were ravaged with leprosy – the 'separating sickness' – which had come about as a result of the increased trading links in the seventeenth century. King Kamehameda V established a leprosarium on the island of Molokai, and in 1866 over 140 sufferers were banished to the island. Here the lepers were isolated and the rest of the population forgot about them.

However, the Catholic Church did not forget them and Bishop Maigret sent Father Joseph to minister to the lepers of Molokai. The plan was to send ministers on a rota basis to help the sufferers, but Father Joseph knew, after just a few days, that he would remain with them, and wrote back: 'I am bent on devoting my life to the lepers. It is absolutely necessary for a priest to live here. The afflicted are coming here by the boatloads.'

For the next 16 years, Father Damien served the growing leper community with Christ-like devotion. He cleaned wounds, bandaged ulcers, amputated gangrenous limbs, built shelters, laid pipelines for fresh water, dug graves and constructed some 1,600 coffins.

Because he lived with these afflicted people and embraced them, it was inevitable that Father Damien himself would contract leprosy. Nevertheless, he did not allow the thought of this to affect his work or faith. In 1888, he enlisted help to set up a girls' orphanage on the island, and three weeks before his ravaged body succumbed to leprosy he was still working hard to comfort his flock. A few days before he died in 1889, he said, 'The work of the lepers is in good hands and I am no longer necessary, so I shall go up yonder.'

On 4 June 1995, Father Joseph was beatified by Pope John Paul II, and today his memory is honoured by a statue that stands in the Rotunda of the US Capitol building. In 1969, when his case was considered for sainthood, Pope Paul VI said of Father Joseph Damien de Veuster: 'Love expresses itself in giving. Saints have not only given of themselves, but they have given of themselves in the service of God and their brethren. Father Damien is certainly in that category. He lived his life of love and dedication in the most heroic yet unassuming way. He lived for others: those whose needs were the greatest.'

THE CURÉ OF ARS

St John Vianney (1786–1859), the Patron of Parish Priests and the Curé of Ars in France, was a poor farmer's son who had much difficulty learning Latin and suffered many illnesses. Although he was ordained by the age of 30, he was considered incapable of leading a parish and needed further training. In short, Vianney had nothing to commend him.

He was very hard on himself but gentle with others. He lived on a diet of boiled potatoes, slept for just two or three hours, and kept himself suspended from the floor by a system of ropes to avoid rats.

However, St John had a remarkable healing ministry and

attracted many people to his services until his fame spread throughout France. A dedicated priest, he would often spend over 15 hours a day hearing confession. He conducted a great struggle against the taverns that encouraged drunkenness and eventually succeeded in banning alcohol in his parish. This is an extract from one of his sermons against the evils of drink:

> St Paul in the Holy Bible assures us that the drunkard will not enter into the kingdom of heaven; drunkenness, therefore, must be a great sin. If drunkenness is a disease:
>
> - It is the only disease contracted by an act of the will
> - It is the only disease that requires a licence to propagate it
> - It is the only disease that is bottled and sold
> - It is the only disease that requires outlets to spread it
> - It is the only disease that produces revenue for the government
> - It is the only disease that is habit forming
> - It is the only disease that produces crime
> - It is the only disease that is permitted to be spread by advertising
> - It is the only disease without a germ or virus and for which there is no corrective medicine
> - It is the only disease that will condemn you to eternal separation from God in Hell. (Gal. 5. 21)

St John Vianney was canonized in 1925. It is said that his body has not decomposed.

THE FATE OF THE APOSTLES

Scripture does not record how the Apostles died, but tradition holds that they were all martyred or banished, as victims of Roman persecution:

Apostle	Cause of death
Peter	Crucified upside down in Rome – AD 66
Andrew	Crucified in AD 74
James, son of Zebedee	Beheaded in Jerusalem – AD 44
John, son of Alphaeus	Beaten to death in AD 60
John the Beloved	Banished to the Isle of Patmos – AD 96
Philip	Crucified in Phryga – AD 52
Bartholomew	Crucified in AD 52
Thomas	Run through by a lance in India – AD 52
Matthew	Slain with a sword in Ethiopia – AD 60
Simon	Crucified in Persia – AD 74
Mark	Died in Alexandria after being dragged through the streets
Thaddaeus	Shot by arrows – AD 72
Paul	Beheaded in Rome – AD 66

THE WIZARD OF BALWEARIE

Little is known for certain about Michael Scot(t), the legendary magician from the twelfth century who lived near Selkirk in Scotland. Tales of his prowess abound, but it is difficult to separate myth from historical fact. It is said that Scot possessed an unparalleled knowledge of magic, philosophy, astronomy, maths and physics. It is claimed he studied at Oxford, Paris, Padua, Bologna and Toledo universities.

He is said to have become a favourite of the Holy Roman

Emperor Frederick II by healing him of an incurable sickness. He was also supposed to own a magical horse that could transport him at fantastic speed from Scotland to Paris. On one occasion, Scot was so tormented by the demon that he commanded it to make rope from the sands of Kirkaldy beach, a task that is never ending!

The wizard's reputation seems largely based on Walter Scott's ballad, 'The Lay of the Last Minstrel', a mention in Dante's *Inferno* (among the magicians and soothsayers), and in a sixteenth-century Italian poem called 'Merlin Coccaius', an extract of which is given below:

Behold renown'd Scotus take his stand
Beneath a tree's deep shadow, and there draw
His magic circle – in its orb describe
Signs, cycles, characters of uncouth shapes;
And with imperious voice his demons call.
Four devils come – one from the golden west,
Another from the east; another still
Sails onwards from the south – and last of all
Arrives the northern devil;

'Tis said that he who wears
His magic cap, invisible may walk,
And none so lynx-eyed as detect his presence,
In the most peopled city – yet beware,
Let him not, trusting to the demon's power,
Cross the white splendour of the sun, for there,
Although no palpable substance is discern'd,
His shadow will betray him.

The Mirror of Literature, Amusement, and Instruction, no. 492, vol. 17, Saturday, 4 June 1831

MAJOR MONASTIC ORDERS

Founder	Order	Habit
St Benedict	BENEDICTINE	Black
St Romualdo	Camaldolesi	White
St Bruno	Carthusians	White
St Bernard of Clairvaux	Cistercians	White
St Bernard dei Tolomei	Olivetani	White
St Philip Neri	Oratorians	Black
St John Gualberto	Vallombrosans	Light grey
St Augustine	AUGUSTINE	Black
St Bridget of Sweden	Brigittines	Black
St Norbert	Premonstratensians	Black or Brown
St Philip Benozzi	Servi	Black
St John de Matha	Trinitarians	White
St Peter Nolasco	Order of Mercy	White
St Albert of Vercelli	CARMELITE	Dark brown
St Theresa	Scalzi	Dark brown
St Dominic	DOMINICAN	White
St Francis of Assisi	FRANCISCAN	Brown or Grey
St Matteo di Bassi	Capuchins	Dark brown
St John of God	Cordeliers	Brown
St Francis de Paula	Minimes	Brown
St Bernardino of Siena	Observants	Grey

St Clara	Poor Clares	Grey or Brown
St Jerome	JERONYMITE	
St Ignatius Loyola	JESUIT	Black
St Francis de Sales	VISITATION OF MARY	Black

CURIOUS SAINTLY DEEDS
– PART FIVE

- St Vitus is the patron saint of dancers and actors and those who find it difficult to get up in the mornings! He was a Sicilian nobleman, who enraged his heathen father by converting to the Christian faith. As punishment he was beaten and cast into a dungeon. But he was attended by angels who danced in the prison in the midst of dazzling light. When the saint's father looked at the scene, he was blinded by the light, but St Vitus' prayers restored his sight. Today, he is noted for a neurological condition called St Vitus Dance (Sydenham's Chorea), characterized by involuntary limb movements and muscle weakness.

- St Zenobius was a fourth-century Bishop of Florence. He had a remarkable ministry of miracles and was much revered by the Florentines. He is said to have restored to life a man who died by falling from a church precipice. On another occasion, a mother brought her dead child to the saint and he prayed and brought the girl back to life. When St Zenobius died, such vast crowds gathered at his grave, to touch him one last time, that his body was pushed against a tree near the cathedral of Florence. The tree, though old and withered, at once produced fresh leaves!

- St Margaret of Cortona lived a wild life in thirteenth-century

Tuscany. She had many lovers, but her life was transformed when one of them was murdered. A little dog guided Margaret to his body and she was so stricken by the sight that she tried to join the Franciscan convent at Cortona. However, they would not receive her because of her sinful past. But one day, when Margaret was praying, she saw Jesus motion towards her and she knew she was forgiven.

- St Charles Borromeo was the Archbishop of Milan in the sixteenth century. When the plague broke out in that city, many fled – but Charles remained to minister to the outcasts. Three times he walked barefoot through the city and, falling before the crucifix in the cathedral, offered himself as a sacrifice for the people. He was a great reformer and campaigned vigorously against religious abuses. Thus he made many enemies, and on one occasion a Franciscan friar fired a shot at him while Charles was at prayer. The bullet got caught in the material of his cape and he survived unharmed!

- St John Nepomuc of Bohemia was the confessor to the wife of Wenceslaus IV, Emperor of Germany in the fourteenth century. The Emperor wanted to know the confessions of his wife, but John refused to tell him. Enraged by his silence, the Emperor had John thrown into the River Moldau. As he sank, five stars in the form of a crown appeared over the spot. St John is the patron saint of silence, running water, bridges and also against slander.

THE PREACHER AND THE PIT

John Wesley, the founder of Methodism, was a famous preacher who covered thousands of miles on horseback to present the gospel throughout Britain. One of his strangest locations was Gwennap Pit, a large hollow formed by the collapse of old underground mines in St Day in Cornwall.

This was the ideal place for meetings because it was sheltered and Wesley's voice could be carried far and wide in the natural amphitheatre. Between 1762 and 1789, John Wesley preached 18 times at Gwennap Pit. The last occasion was when he was 86 and he recorded in his diary, 'I preached in the amphitheatre I suppose for the last time; for my voice cannot command the still increasing multitudes . . .'

Gwennap Pit became a popular open air 'pulpit' for many preachers after Wesley's death. Today, Methodists from around the world still gather at the Pit for the annual Whit Monday service and it has even been the location for a few wedding ceremonies!

SAINTS' AND SINNERS' QUOTES

The revealed truth of the Bible is not that Jesus Christ took on Himself our fleshly sins, but that He took on Himself the heredity of sin. God made His own Son 'to be sin' that He might make the sinner into a saint.

Oswald Chambers, My Utmost for His Highest

The only difference between the saint and the sinner is that every saint has a past, and every sinner has a future.

Oscar Wilde, A Woman of No Importance

Grace is indeed needed to turn a man into a saint; and he who doubts it does not know what a saint is.

Blaise Pascal, Pensées

Can one be a saint without God? This is the only problem I know of today.

Albert Camus, La Peste

Many of the insights of the saint stem from his experience as a sinner.

Eric Hoffer, The Passionate State of Mind

Many people genuinely do not wish to be saints, and it is probable that some who achieve or aspire to sainthood have never felt much temptation to be human beings.

George Orwell, Shooting an Elephant

I fear that Christians who stand with only one leg upon earth also stand with only one leg in heaven.

Dietrich Bonhoeffer, letter to his fiancée, 1943

Christians have burnt each other, quite persuaded
That all the Apostles would have done as they did

Lord Byron, Don Juan

Christ beats his drum, but he does not press men; Christ is served with voluntaries.

John Donne, Sermons, no. 39

He that will not live as a saint, can never die a martyr.

Thomas Fuller, Gnomologia

Men die only for that by which they live.

Saint-Exupéry, Flight to Arras
The International Thesaurus of Quotations,
ed. Rhoda Thomas Tripp, Penguin, 1970

SAINTS AND THEIR FLOWERS

For centuries, the *sanctorale*, the calendar of saints, provided a useful way of marking the natural passing of the seasons and the agricultural year. Many saints were remembered by association with what the land produced at the time of their martyrdom. This is an early English church calendar giving the flowers linked to saints and their feast days:

> While the Crocus hastens to the shrine
> Of Primrose love on St Valentine
> Then comes the daffodil, besides
> Our Ladyes-Smock at our Ladye-tide.
> About St George, when blue is worn,
> The blue Harebells the fields adorn;
> Against the daie of Holie Cross,
> The Crowfoot gilds the flowerie grasse.
> When Barnabie bright smiles night and daie,
> Poor Ragged Robin blossoms in the haie.
> The Scarlet Lynchnis, the garden pride,
> Flames at St John the Baptist's tide.
> From Visitation to St Swithin's showers,
> Lilie White reigns Queen of the floures.
> And Poppies, a sanguine mantle spred,
> For the blood of the dragon St Margaret shed.
> Then under the wanton Rose, again
> That blushes for Penitent Magdalen.
> Till Lammas daie, called August's Wheel,
> When the long corn stinks of Cammamile,
> When Mary left us here belowe,
> The Virgin's Bower is fullin blaw;
> And yet anon, the full Sunfloure blew,
> And became a starre, for Bartholomew.
> The Passion-Floure long has blowed,
> To betoken us signs of the Holy Roode . . .
> The Michaelmas Daisies, among dede weeds,
> Blooms for St Michael's valorous deeds.

And seems the last of floures that stroude,
Till the feste of St Simon and St Jude.
Save Mushrooms and the Fungus race,
That grow till All-Hallow-tide take place.
Soon the ever-green Laurel alone is greene,
When Catherine crowns all learned menne.
The Ivie and Holly berries are seen,
And Yule-log and wassails come round agen.

Flora Sancta, *Norwich, Canterbury Press*

CURIOUS SAINTLY DEEDS
– PART SIX

- St William of Bourges, who died in 1207, always wore a hair-shirt and never ate meat. When he was dying, he asked for his body to be laid on ashes in his hair-shirt. His relics were venerated for over 300 years and supposed to work many miracles. It is said that a bone of his arm is still at Chaalis in France, and one of his ribs at Paris.

- St Ulrick, who died in 1154, was born near Bristol. He became a priest, and kept dogs and hawks for sport, till he met a beggar who asked for alms. When Ulrick said he didn't know if he had anything to give, the beggar said, 'Look in thy purse, and you shall find twopence halfpenny.' He found as he was told and gave it to the beggar, who prophesied that Ulrick would become a saint. He was a hermit, fasting often, at Hessleborough in Dorset. He never slept unless he could not stay awake, and slept leaning against a wall. Waking up, he would chastise his body for being so lazy. After a hair-shirt became too comfortable, he changed it for an iron coat of mail. In winter he sat in a tub of cold water reciting psalms.

- St Vincent was a Spanish martyr said to have been tormented by fire, so that he died in 304. His body was thrown in a marshy field among rushes, but a crow defended it from wild beasts and birds of prey. Tradition records that the crow drove away birds and fowls greater than himself, and that it chased a wolf with his beak.

- Jesuit accounts record that Emperor Alexander IV wanted St Martina as his wife. She refused him, so the Emperor commanded her to be tortured. The Jesuits' stories of these operations and her escapes are wonderfully particular. According to them, hooks and stakes did her no mischief; she had a faculty of shining, which the pouring of hot oil upon her would not quench; when in gaol, men in dazzling white surrounded her; she could not feel 118 wounds; a fierce lion, who had fasted three days, would not eat her, and fire would not burn her; but a sword cut her head off in 228, and at the end of two days two eagles were found watching her body.

- St Mildred was the first Abbess of Minster, in the Isle of Thanet, founded by King Egbert in about 670. The Minster was built by command of the King to expiate his murder of his two nephews, Etheldred and Ethelbright. Mildred's relics were taken St Augustine's monastery at Canterbury in 1033. They were venerated above all the relics there, and worked many miracles. The churches of St Mildred, Bread Street, and St Mildred in the Poultry, London, are dedicated to her.

CURIOUS DEEDS OF
ENGLISH SAINTS

- St Elphege (or Alphege) became Bishop of Winchester in 1006 and Archbishop of Canterbury. He was imprisoned in Greenwich by the Danes who overran Kent and London in 1011. While in prison the devil appeared to him in likeness of an angel, and tempted him to follow him into a dark valley, over which he wearily walked through hedges and ditches. At last the devil vanished, and a real angel appeared and told St Alphege to be a martyr. He was slain by the Danes in 1012 and is buried in St Paul's in London.

- St John of Beverley was Bishop of Hexham, a village in the North of England. Several miracles are related to him, including his ability to calm fierce bulls and healing oil issuing from his sepulchre in 1312. He is also supposed to have inspired King Ethelstan to victory over the Scots.

- St Aldhelm founded the Abbey of Malmesbury, and was the first Englishman to cultivate both Latin and English. He lived a life of strict discipline and used to recite the psalter at night, plunged up to the shoulders in a pond of water. His biographers say that while in Rome he turned a sunbeam into a clothes-peg to hang his vestments! He died in 709.

- Bede's *Ecclesiastical History* records St Alban as being the first martyr (in 303) in Britain. Alban was from Verulamium (now the town of St Albans) in Hertfordshire. He is supposed to have converted his executioner, caused a river to dry up, and a fountain to appear on the summit of the hill where he was executed.

- St Walburg (or Walburga) was born in 710, in Devonshire, the daughter of King Richard, sister of St Willibald and St Winebald. In 748, she left England to evangelize Germany as part of St Boniface's mission. She had amazing skills of healing and is the patron saint of those afflicted by plague, rabies and coughs.

- St Chad was born in 673 and became the founder and bishop of the see of Lichfield. He is famous for blessing a local well that offered miraculous cures, causing thousands of people to crowd to the site. According to Bede, before the saint died, there was 'joyful melody as of persons sweetly singing descended from heaven for half an hour, and then mounted again to heaven'.